made in canada

CRAFT AND DESIGN IN THE SIXTIES

edited by **ALAN C. ELDER**

Published for **Design Exchange**, Toronto, in collaboration with
the **Canadian Museum of Civilization** by

McGill-Queen's University Press
Montreal & Kingston | London | Ithaca

© McGill-Queen's University Press 2005

ISBN 0-7735-2873-3

Legal deposit first quarter 2005
Bibliothèque nationale du Québec

Printed in Canada on acid-free paper

McGill-Queen's University Press acknowledges the support of the Canada Council
for the Arts for our publishing program. We also acknowledge the financial
support of the Government of Canada through the Book Publishing Industry
Development Program (BPIDP) for our publishing activities.

This publication is supported by the Department of Canadian
Heritage Museums Assistance Program.

LIBRARY AND ARCHIVES CANADA CATALOGUING IN PUBLICATION

Made in Canada: craft and design in the sixties / edited by Alan C. Elder.

ISBN 0-7735-2873-3

1. Handicraft – Canada – History – 20th century.   2. Design – Canada – History –
20th century.   3. Nineteen sixties.   4. Handicraft – Government policy – Canada –
History – 20th century.   5. Design – Government policy – Canada – History – 20th century.
6. Popular culture – Canada – History – 20th century.   I. Elder, Alan C., 1955–
II. Canadian Museum of Civilization   III. Design Exchange (Firm)

NK1413.A1M34 2005   745'.0971'09046   C2004-906154-2

Chapter 5, "Habitat '67: View from the Inside" by Paul Bourassa,
was translated from the French by Phyllis Aronoff and Howard Scott.

Cover: Chair by Ebena-Lasalle
Collection of the Canadian Museum of Civilization, CMCC-2004.56.1
Photo: Harry Foster, Canadian Museum of Civilization

CONTENTS

CANADA WELCOMES THE WORLD

SAME DECADE, DIFFERENT STYLES

When I was in kindergarten in 1967, my class was given red crayons and the mimeographed image of the Canadian maple leaf flag, which we were told to colour in. What wasn't very well explained to us was that this was a *new* flag that had been designed, in the Canadian manner, by committee, just in time for the country's centenary. In hindsight, I can see that my somewhat elderly teacher probably loathed this new flag. She likely believed that the old flag – baronial and ornate, with a Union Jack and lots of doodads – was the real thing, not this reductive glyph that seemed more like a corporate logo than something to be flown at the Legion Hall.

Aside from the flag experience, I actually remember very little of the sixties, but not in the hippie sense of forgetting – I was simply too young. Those cultural memories I do have along with the flag memory are murky: Vietnam on the old black and white TV, new music from the Beatles, and, thankfully, Expo 67 – particularly the U.S. pavilion's geodesic dome and the Moshe Safdie modular housing. What I'm now realizing is that while exuberant modernism was business as usual to young people like myself, to older Canadians Expo was something else. It marked a cathartic and definitive breaking away from the Canadian past. No longer was the nation's visual identity going to be defined by styles or expressions that were either too regional or too historically problematic. Modern was incontestably better, although again I return to the new flag of 1965. I remember my parents railing on about it and how awful it was (and in their mind, still is). I've never been too fond of it, not because I think it's unattractive, but rather – and I figured this out in kindergarten – because it's undrawable. I've had a series of parties recently where a total of over a hundred guests were handed a red felt pen and asked to draw a maple leaf on a wall slated for demolition. Most of the results resembled fig or marijuana leaves. Not one guest – all of them adults who'd grown up with the maple leaf – came close. The larger point being made here is that post offices and mailboxes swapped their ornate undrawable coats of arms for an equally undrawable reductive modernism motif. *Plus ça change ...*

But the sixties are now a long time ago, so long ago that younger generations don't realize what they're doing when they loot it for style cues and ideas. The sixties are officially history, and for the first time we have the historical distance to be reasonably objective about much of what happened then, design included. Forty years later we can look at Canada's attempt to define its sense of mythic self without sentimentality as almost sentimental in itself. Like those old teen movies of the era, instead of *Hey Gang! Let's put on a show!*, it was more like, *Hey Gang! Let's put on a country!*

The sixties were also a point when there was no possibility of going in reverse, only forward, and quickly, sometimes too quickly. I may have been five and a half when I visited Expo, but I clearly remember its built-ten-minutes-ago aura. All of those shiny pavilion walls that look so sexy in photos were, up close, pretty sterile. And this isn't a put-down – it's a way of illustrating how fast change was happening. World's fairs are intrinsically like stage sets, and while I do remember being on the monorail there and saying to myself, *It's like floating above a parking lot*, I was also aware that most of the islands on which Expo was built were only a year or two older than the fair. I remember being told that we Canadians now inhabited an era of designed super-projects. Here was the proof. A recent trip back to the fair site was odd for me. It felt like time travel gone wrong. Many of the pavilions whose lifespan was to have been only a year or so have been kept on architectural life-support. The fair's temporality was revealed with depressing force. Something that so forcibly moulded the memories of tens of millions of citizens now had only the power to depress.

The sixties marked another large change for Canada. After being industrially crippled by the Imperial Preference System – a trade agreement that essentially treated Canada as a goose from which Mother Britain could endlessly pluck golden eggs – the former colony was clearly manufacturing and marketing items on its own. While shadows of the IPS system cripple Canada to this day, the sixties at least began to offer Canadians a whiff of hope that they might one day get off the raw materials treadmill. Exuberant new designs deflated old and defeated ways of thinking. To look through an Eaton's catalogue from the era is to see generational warfare played out in the nation's clothing and furniture departments. Just how the department stores managed to inventory this clash of sensibilities is hard to comprehend.

It's also important to remember that the sixties were the decade when the focus shifted to urban life, creating the tendency to sentimentalize the land and the out-of-doors. Raw materials, in the form of the land and its abundance, became liberating, and Canadian design of the times seems to have revelled in that abundance. Massive structures made of undiluted and roughly hewn chunks of metals and woods were a way of waving goodbye to the past and of postulating an almost James Bond future of style through excess. When our family moved to Vancouver in 1965, we lived on a street now regarded as a design laboratory and considered required visiting for architectural students. Back then, all I wanted was a house with dormer windows like the families on TV had. Now I look at the sixties houses and wonder if I could afford to ever live in one. They've aged very gracefully.

I also grew up skiing, back when it was dirt cheap and not the sport of kings. This is important because the architecture and design of skiing are intrinsically sixties. They marry together high technology and new materials with the rusticity of the mountain and generous helpings of the raw materials found there. In 1964, the Canadian pavilion at the Triennale di Milano was a cottage – designed by Ottawa architect Paul Schoeler. Within this "roughing it in the bush" environment was a stereo much like the one featured in *The Graduate.* Here the concept of "big nature" was tempered by a sophisticated Clairtone Project G stereo.

The whole notion of the "decade" is arbitrary, although it's true that decades sometimes make for good bookends for specific cultural moments. Our culture's obsession with decades intensified in the sixties, possibly because the decade itself was so clearly a decade, one that saw the fruition of many ideas vital to the continued vitality of the country – a distinct location in global politics and a continuing debate about geographical and ideological unity.

I look at it this way: I'm 43 this year and Canada is 137, which means that I've been around for nearly 31 per cent of the nation's official existence. My father has been around for 57 per cent of the country's existence. Those are big numbers. I've said it before and I'll say it again: Canada is a young country and it has yet to become what it is ultimately going to be. Unlike many countries, we still have the power to control our future. It's what unifies us, and recognition of this fact was perhaps the greatest sixties design of all.

And I still wish our flag were easier to draw.

Douglas Coupland

Design Exchange (DX) is honoured to participate in this important publication. *Made in Canada: Craft and Design in the Sixties* is an exciting initiative and reflects an important part of Canada's design history.

Our collaboration with the Canadian Museum of Civilization helps us fulfil our mandate: first, to build public awareness of the importance of design in creating Canada's cultural identity, and second, to increase the number of globally competitive products and services designed and made in Canada.

DX has three areas of focus: museum, education and research. In our Resource Centre, we are delighted to house the only permanent collection solely devoted to Canadian industrial design, dating from 1945 to the present, as well as an extensive design archive and library. One of our collection's most exciting objects, the Lollipop seating system designed by Robin Bush, is featured in this book and the accompanying exhibition. Although many artifacts of Canadian design have been neglected or destroyed, there remains nonetheless a tremendous opportunity to reclaim our design history and to recognize landmark achievements as they happen.

Our education programs are strong and target elementary school, high school, and post-secondary students. Frequent tours of the DX Resource Centre offer students a glimpse of some of the most celebrated objects in our collection from the sixties, such as the Project G stereo and the Ball-B-Q. Additionally, we host annual competitions for students and professionals to nurture excellence in all disciplines.

Our research includes design industry issues such as sustainability and economic impact, and our publications are distributed to the educational and professional communities. Through these areas of focus, we fulfil our mandate and expand the knowledge base in Canada and internationally.

Efforts such as this publication require many dedicated staff and partnerships. Funding from the Department of Canadian Heritage Museums Assistance Program was critical in developing this publication and is much appreciated. We also wish to thank McGill-Queen's University Press for their generous support. For their tremendous effort, enthusiasm, and cooperative spirit, it is an honour to thank Alan Elder, the Canadian Museum of Civilization's first curator of craft and design, and Design Exchange's Elise Hodson, director of exhibitions.

Samantha Sannella
President and CEO, Design Exchange

FOREWORD
Canadian Museum of Civilization

The sixties were years of dynamic change in Canada, brought about in part through a creative interplay between many individuals, organizations, and governments. This publication and the exhibition that it documents, *Cool '60s Design*, revisits the spirit of innovation and collaboration that marked this exceptional time.

In 2002 the Canadian Museum of Civilization joined a multi-institutional partnership to re-examine the sixties. Montreal's Museum of Fine Arts, the Canadian Centre for Architecture, the McCord Museum, the National Gallery of Canada, and the Canadian Museum of Contemporary Photography joined with us to present a series of events on this exciting decade. The extent of this co-operation around a specific cultural theme was unprecedented. It echoed the spirit of the sixties and, perhaps, might become a model for future cultural collaboration.

When the Canadian Museum of Civilization began discussions with Toronto's Design Exchange (DX) about our plans for an exhibition of Canadian craft and design, DX staff members – particularly Elise Hodson – were enthusiastic. This book, *Made in Canada: Craft and Design in the Sixties*, is the result of our collaborative effort. Writers from various parts of the country, all with different expertise, have worked with the museum's Alan C. Elder and DX staff to elaborate on the themes in the exhibition. The museum also provided publication photographs taken by Harry Foster, our manager of photographic services, as well as production assistance.

The Canadian Museum of Civilization explores issues, collects artifacts, and presents exhibitions and programs on Canadian themes that deal with history and contemporary society. Many of these themes are examined through the material objects that we encounter in our daily routines or special events. One exceptional period was Canada's centennial in 1967, highlighted by the Montreal World's Fair (Expo 67), which expressed and celebrated Canada's transformed modernity. Our exhibition, *Cool '6os Design*, and this book look again at the everyday material objects that met the demands of Canadians – objects designed, crafted, and made in Canada.

Victor Rabinovitch
President and CEO, Canadian Museum of Civilization Corporation

made in canada

INTRODUCTION

Canada in the Sixties –
"It can do almost anything"

ALAN C. ELDER

*We are being pushed and pushed hard by a unique generation: the first generation raised
with television, the first generation raised in a secular age, the first generation raised with
the Bomb. If it is a mixed-up generation – "cool" and at the same time committed;
hedonistic and at the same time idealistic – it is also remarkably self-possessed.*[1]

While there is much discussion about the birth date of an independent Canadian nation – some say it was Confederation, others Vimy Ridge, and still others
World War II – many cultural historians agree that the nation came of age in
the sixties. And at the same time as the nation came of age, so did the baby
boomers. The exuberant naiveté of sixties youth culture lost its innocence
during the unrest of the decade's latter years.

Pierre Berton has lamented that 1967 was Canada's "Last Good Year."[2]
Canada's centennial celebrations had projected an image of a modern Canadian
nation onto film and television screens around the world. Peter C. Newman
wrote of the opening day of Expo 67 in the *Toronto Star*: "The more you see of
it, the more you're overwhelmed by a feeling that if this is possible, that if
this little sub-arctic, self-obsessed country of 20,000,000 people can put on this
kind of show, then it can do almost anything."[3] But these celebrations marked
the end of an era as well as a beginning. The year that followed – 1968 – proved
to be a year of global change and unrest. Students around the world protested
the powers of government and industry. The struggle for individual rights

– a struggle that continues today – erupted immediately after Canada's year-long birthday party.

Made in Canada: Craft and Design in the Sixties addresses the federal government's initiatives to redesign the nation through the adoption of legislation that was aimed at creating a vital, new national identity. Included in these initiatives were the development of modern air terminals across the country, the adoption of a new flag, and Expo 67. *Made in Canada* also looks at the impact that government initiatives had on contemporaneous culture. The launch of the space satellite, *Alouette 1*, in 1962, for instance, prompted the transformation of everyday goods into space-age forms. At the same time, the success of *Alouette 1* turned up the heat on discussions of communications theory – particularly by Canada's guru of the sixties, Marshall McLuhan (Figure 1.1). In *Mondo Canuck: A Canadian Pop Culture Odyssey*, Geoff Pevere and Craig Dymond posit this equation: "Consider This: '60s Britain = Music and fashion. '60s America = Music and politics. '60s France = Culture and politics. '60s Canada = Media Theorists."[4] Our geography forced us to adopt new ways of relating with others, within Canada and outside.

This volume also addresses the demise of a singular, and serious, conceptualization of modern life – as was seen in the immediate postwar period – and its replacement with a focus on popular culture and consumerism. The concept of "good design," which public institutions and manufacturers had espoused, was replaced with new, streetwise, and varied sensibilities. These sensibilities aligned individuals according to their interests rather than by age, gender, or ethnicity – what today would be labelled "psychographics." Groups of like-thinking Canadians developed specific approaches to life. Many Canadians adopted clothing and furniture styles developed on London's Carnaby Street. A pop lifestyle featured go-go dancing, bold colours and prints, and a fondness for synthetic materials that had become affordable as patents on familiar plastics ran out and new, less expensive ones were developed. Some Canadians pursued an interest in modernity – but this was no longer a hard-edged modernism with utopian goals; instead it was based on an increasing knowledge of the advantages and disadvantages of modernization. No longer were individuals unaware of the implications of new technologies and unbridled uses of natural resources. Another group, also concerned with the ecological impact of consumer society, was unhappy with the role that "big" governments had taken; they voiced their concerns in public rallies and demonstrations, and reinforced

FIGURE I.1

Marshall McLuhan (centre), wearing a blazer and tie made from Maple Leaf tartan fabric designed by David Weiser in 1965, with Dick Martin (left) and Dan Rowan of television's *Laugh-In*.

their commitment to the environment by reusing materials and relearning traditional practices. Handcrafted items played a particularly important role in the creation of a grassroots culture.

Made in Canada: Craft and Design in the Sixties, together with the exhibition – *Cool '60s Design* – that it accompanies, brings together ideas of national dreams and expressions of individuality by juxtaposing photographic documentation of the decade with texts by experts from across the country. The volume, illustrated throughout with contemporary images of objects that were made in Canada during the sixties, consists of three interrelated components, each reflecting an important socio-cultural issue or event that affected the look of objects made in Canada.

The first, "Designing a Modern Nation," with essays about the Canadian maple leaf flag, Canada's entry into the space race, and the development of air terminals across the country, investigates the impact of government initiatives on Canadian design. The Canadian government was interested in recreating Canada as a modern nation. Buoyed by Canada's role in World War II, the government undertook programs that utilized modern design as a way of projecting an up-to-date and sophisticated image of the country in the minds of Canadians and people around the world.

In his essay, "When 'la Dolce Vita' Met 'True Canadianism': Canadian Airports in the Sixties," Regina-based architect Bernard Flaman looks at the work of Canada's Department of Transport as it began to redevelop air terminals across the country in the late 1950s, starting in Gander, Newfoundland. The program continued to develop throughout the sixties, with the opening of terminals in Halifax, Montreal, Ottawa, Toronto, Winnipeg, Edmonton and finally Vancouver. This series of airports incorporated modern architecture, furniture design, crafts, and fine arts – all working together to create modern gateways to the nation for travellers, particularly international visitors and immigrants to Canada. As Flaman notes, these glass curtain–walled structures, filled with art, craft, and design from across the country, met with varied responses from individuals and organizations. Many questioned whether the terminals should address national or local concerns. This discussion has resonance today as new terminals, developed by local authorities, replace those federal initiatives of the sixties.

In 1962 Canada became the third nation to enter the space race when *Alouette 1* was launched. Toronto-based design curator Rachel Gotlieb's essay, "'Instant World': Canada and Space-Age Design in the Sixties," investigates the role of

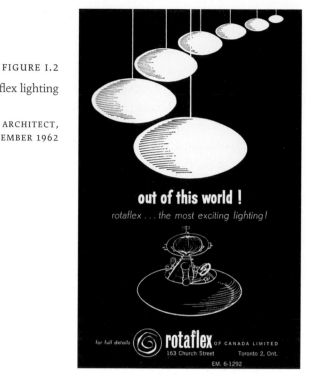

Alouette 1 and its legacy. The federal government made it clear that its entry into space was for peaceful purposes, differentiating its program from that of the United States and the Soviet Union. Canada's legacy in the development of satellite communications was of particular importance in a country where a relatively small population was, and continues to be, spread across a large geographic area. Today, discussion of communications has shifted its emphasis from telephone and television to the Internet, yet many of the same concerns are expressed, especially regarding universal access to technology. The space race altered the design of Canadian-made objects. Electrohome, a maker of electronics in Kitchener, Ontario, designed and made a series of stereo systems that embodied futurist design motifs. As well, a lighting manufacturer in Toronto – Rotaflex – developed an advertising campaign that claimed that its products were "out of this world!" (Figure I.2).

In his election campaign of 1963, Lester Pearson promised that Canada would have a flag of its own within two years. An all-party committee of the House of Commons examined almost six thousand proposals, many of them submitted by artists and designers. After animated public debate, a single red maple leaf was chosen to represent Canada as an independent and unified nation. In his essay, "A Flag for Canada," graphic design historian Michael Large, associate dean for design programs at Oakville's Sheridan College, writes about what was probably the most influential Canadian design from the sixties: the Canadian flag. The move from the use of the Red Ensign to the maple leaf was a controversial one – a political question based on issues of aesthetics and identity. Canadians from across the country debated Canada's alliances with both Britain and France and its development as a multicultural society. A logical outgrowth of the design for a Canadian flag was the development of the Federal Identity Program – the familiar "Canada" wordmark that has branded federal government departments and activities since the late sixties and that can even be seen in space on the Canadarm.

This volume's second section, "Canada Welcomes the World," showcases Expo 67 in Montreal. In her book *The Sixties: Decade of Design Revolution*, design historian Lesley Jackson states that "[it] could be argued, in fact, that the Expo was the culmination of 'the look' of the early Sixties, and that 1967 marked at once a high point and a turning point in design."[5] Expo was also an opportunity for Canada – and for the city of Montreal – to present itself to the world as sophisticated and up to date. Canadian planners, architects, artists, designers and craftspeople were brought together on two islands – mostly artificially made – in the St Lawrence River to create an environment that would surround the visitor with cutting-edge design and technology. Two aspects of craft and design at the Montreal World's Fair are addressed in this volume. One addresses the place of craft in relation to other visual arts, while the other looks at Habitat '67, an icon of the fair, Montreal, and the sixties (Figure 1.3).

The first aspect of Expo 67 is addressed by Halifax-based craft historian and professor Sandra Alfoldy in her essay, "Excellence, Inventiveness, and Variety: *Canadian Fine Crafts* at Expo 67." The Canadian government's pavilion at the fair, probably best known for its inverted pyramidal *Katimavik*, included a gallery building. Here the government showcased the country's best visual artists in the fine arts, architecture, photography, and craft. The *Painting in Canada* exhibition included works by Cornelius Krieghoff, Tom Thomson, and Jean-Paul Riopelle

FIGURE I.3

Moshe Safdie in front of Montreal's Habitat '67 during construction, 1966

among others; the photography exhibition focused on the work of Karsh; and the architecture display featured buildings by John Parkin and Arthur Erickson. Alongside these exhibitions was a display of Canadian craft. Moncrieff Williamson assembled the exhibition and later arranged for some of the works to be purchased for the collection of the Confederation Centre in Charlottetown, where he was the director of the art gallery. Alfoldy's essay problematizes the place of Canadian craft at Expo and its collection by the Confederation Centre. The legacy of craft collections is still being debated as institutions revisit their collection policies and question the place of the applied arts (Figure 1.4).

In his essay, "Habitat '67: A View from the Inside," design historian Paul Bourassa, from the Musée national des beaux-arts de Québec, investigates the role of design in Moshe Safdie's groundbreaking building. Habitat '67 was a continuation of Canadian experiments in providing high-density housing within an urban context at a reasonable price. As the size of the project was scaled down and its costs continually rose, it became an exclusive residence. But during Expo, it was also a showcase for interiors by a number of Canadian designers. Safdie, along with Montreal's Jacques Guillon, had to lobby the Expo commissioners to involve Canadian designers in the furnishing of twelve model suites. With only months to prepare and virtually no budget, these designers created interiors that were as unique as the housing complex itself. The short lead-time meant that some designers had to use recent existing designs. Other designers created new furniture for Habitat, many featuring a boxy modularity similar to the building itself. Posed on Mackay Pier opposite the city, Habitat remains an icon of its time and place.

The third, and final, component of this volume turns away from the two previous elements. Rather than investigate the role of the modern Canadian government, "Same Decade, Different Styles" looks at the increasingly important role of the individual, particularly as the decade was coming to an end. In his book *The Cool, Crazy, Committed World of the Sixties*, Pierre Berton states, "The Sixties became the decade of The New Left and The New Morality, The New Frankness and The New Concern. In these Go-Go years, we have heard the drums of revolution sound in almost every arena."[6] The sixties were a time of increasing affluence and enormous social upheaval in Canada. Issues as disparate as Quebec separatism, women's liberation, homosexuality, and First Nations rights demonstrated the diversity of emerging identities. Unhappy with the status quo, the large number of baby boomers who came of age in the

FIGURE I.4

Robert Oldrich, *Flower Vase*, 1966 (enamel on metal)

COLLECTION OF
CONFEDERATION CENTRE OF
THE ARTS, CHARLOTTETOWN,
CM 67.1.43

PHOTO: CAMERA ART –
CHARLOTTETOWN

COURTESY OF HELGA AND
DIETER MOLL

sixties demanded that manufacturers supply them with goods that met their personal lifestyles. The final component of this volume examines three different approaches to life in the "Go-Go years."

In his essay "Capsules: Plastic and Utopia," Toronto designer and educator Brent Cordner investigates an iconic material of Canadian design in the sixties – plastic. Nowhere was the influence of popular culture on design more evident. In the sixties, many patents for plastic products ran out, making plastic goods inexpensive to produce and therefore available to a wide range of individuals. Simultaneously, the severity of postwar modern design was replaced with an exuberant pop aesthetic, best exemplified by the plastic interior of Montreal's Le Drug, designed by François Dallegret. Because of their easy availability and their allusion to an up-to-date "swinging" style, plastic furniture and furnishings were made for Canadians in every income bracket and age. Plastic lamps, plastic chairs, plastic tables, and plastic dressers were produced by Canadian companies but were related – aesthetically and in mode of production – to the wares made in other countries. Today, as they focus on international rather than domestic markets, Canadian manufacturers are revisiting pop sensibilities in the design of contemporary objects (Figure 1.5).

Some Canadians, particularly those with more established incomes and careers, preferred a more cautious approach to innovation. They were attracted to a warm, livable style that was also serious, elegant, and tasteful. Michael Prokopow, curator, Design Exchange, and professor, Ryerson University, examines a style that was sometimes called the "international look" in Canadian furniture in his essay "Deign to Be Modern: Canada's Taste for Scandinavian Design in the Sixties." In the sixties, this look was thought to be the result of public demand for greater freedom and variety in décor. As well, the press at the time claimed that it was the outcome of Canadians becoming increasingly international in outlook, in everything from cars to architecture.[7] The modified version of modernism adopted by these individuals was greatly influenced by popular Scandinavian designs of the day, particularly those made of teak.

Finally, some Canadians rejected the consumerist approach of their fellow citizens. Some of these individuals had come to Canada as support for American involvement in the war in Vietnam declined. They often lived communally and made what they needed for everyday living – baking bread, dyeing cloth, making furniture and pots – eschewing the consumerist approach of others. In "When Counterculture Went Mainstream," I look at the way that rejection

Avant-Garde 2000—A Plastic Odyssey

Discover Avant-Garde and express the feelings of your generation. Get onto the new concept—stark simplicity of design. You don't have to babysit with this collection: made of Cycolac (ABS thermoplastic) it resists bumps, mars, stains and alcohol marks. Now, explore and enjoy a journey through the suites.

1 to 7 The bedroom. Look forward to these pieces that cut cleaning down to one wipe of a damp cloth. Drawer fronts come in a choice of two colours. State headboard width on order.

8 to 12 The dining room. Weighted bases keep tables stable. Chairs are stackable. You get unique interchangeable green and fuchsia drawer fronts with the buffet. So, go ahead and change your colour scheme when you're in the mood. Forget about hours of cleaning—just run a damp cloth over these very tough pieces and free your mind for better things.

Bedroom—pick a piece or build a suite. Drawered pieces only. *Colours: order by number and name. 59-fuchsia; 39-green.* Headboards, beds and mirror frames come in white only.

Key	Item	Size in inches	Cat. No.	Each
(1)	Triple dresser base, 6 drawers	62 x 20 x 28 high	F70-A 4110C	134.95
	Double dresser base, 4 drawers	42 x 20 x 28 high	F70-A 4109C	114.95
(2)	Vertical mirror	21 x 47 high	F70-A 4111	39.95
(3)	Six-drawer chest	22 x 20 x 51 high	F70-A 4112C	114.95
(4)	Night table	22 x 20 x 22 high	F70-A 4116C	59.95
(5)	Headboard	State 39, 60 wide	F70-A 4114A	39.95
(6)	Student desk, 2 drawers	46 x 20 x 29 high	F70-A 4113C	104.95
(7)	Cruiser bed with 231 coil type quilt top mattress	39 wide	F70-A 4115	124.95

These items are shipped directly from factory.

White dining room pieces and suites. Chairs only. *Colours: order by number and name. 70-white; 09-red.*

Key	Item	Size in inches	Cat. No.	Each
(8)	Round table	48 diam.	F70-A 1026	99.95
	Round table	40 diam.	F70-A 1004	89.95
(9)	Carton of 4 chairs		F70-A 1023C	85.00
	Carton of 2 chairs		F70-A 1022C	43.00
(10)	Buffet, 3 doors, 3 drawers	62 x 20 x 35 high	F70-A 1019	189.95

Five-piece suite, 48" round white table, four chairs.
F70-A 1024CE—State chair colour choice—Suite **179.95**
Five-piece suite, 40" round white table, four chairs.
F70-A 1021CE—State chair colour choice—Suite **169.95**
Smoked pieces and suites. Tables only have rosewood colour tops.

Key	Item	Size in ins	Cat. No.	Each
(11)	Round table	40 diam.	F70-A 1016	99.95
	Round table	48 diam.	F70-A 1027	114.95
(12)	Carton of 4 chairs		F70-A 1018	95.00
	Carton of 2 chairs		F70-A 1017	48.00

Five-piece suite, 40" round table, four chairs.
F70-A 1015E—Suite **189.95**
Five-piece suite, 48" round table, four chairs.
F70-A 1025E—Suite **199.95**

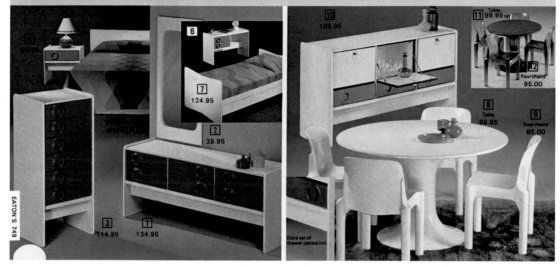

FIGURE I.5

Giovanni Maur, Avant-Garde 2000 furniture for Treco Ltd, 1968 (ABS plastic)

FROM EATON'S CATALOGUE, SPRING/SUMMER 1973
COLLECTION OF ARCHIVES OF ONTARIO, F229-1-0-327
COURTESY OF SEARS CANADA INC.

of the status quo galvanized a group in its rediscovery of artistic traditions. Today, environmental concerns are again coming to the forefront, providing an opportunity for the development of "green" products. Simultaneously, we are becoming increasingly concerned with the anonymity of urban life, and are looking at ways to develop new concepts for communities.

The eight essays included in this volume offer various snapshots of the ways that craft and design affected the lives of Canadians and the ways that Canadians altered craft and design in the sixties. As with any collection of essays, it is impossible to include all aspects of a particular subject. It is my hope that these essays will allow the reader to learn about the increasing importance of modernism in Canadian craft and design in the sixties, as well as about how the Canadian government utilized modernism as a way of representing the nation as autonomous and sophisticated.

The contributors to this book help us understand the birth of what would now be labelled "identity politics." The sixties witnessed an increasing awareness of the role of the individual, and this extended to an awareness that individuals are active agents in the design of their surroundings. Finally, this volume gives us an opportunity to look back at a period that began with optimism and ended with widespread distrust. Today, after a period in which post-modernism broadly degraded the modern project, we can now reconsider many aspects of the sixties in Canada by looking at the material culture that has been left behind. *Made in Canada* provides us with an opportunity to reassess a time when the concerns of the society – those of Canada – met those of individuals – Canadians themselves.

designing a modern nation

I

When "la Dolce Vita" Met "True Canadianism": Canadian Airports in the Sixties

BERNARD FLAMAN

A half-century ago, Canada's air terminals were an embarrassment to the nation. According to a 1957 *Globe and Mail* article quoted two years later in *Canadian Architect*:

Canada's international airports, "which provide many through-travellers with their only view of Canada and many immigrants with their first look at this prosperous country, are squalid." Malton airport in Toronto was a "national disgrace"; Dorval, "tight, tawdry, tumultuous"; Gander, "a poor advertisement for Canada"; Winnipeg, "totally inadequate."[1]

Canadian Architect also quoted *Saturday Night* magazine's 1958 citation that Canadian airport buildings were "undoubtedly among the world's worst."[2]

Between 1952 and 1968, Canada's Department of Transport moved to address the problem by building a nationwide air-terminal infrastructure that entailed the construction of twenty-two new buildings.[3] Architecturally, these exemplary buildings shared common modernist themes, and within they boasted the latest Canadian and international furniture. Evoking the atmosphere of an art gallery, the interior spaces displayed the largest public art project ever realized in Canada.[4] With the guidance of the National Gallery of Canada, the Department of Transport commissioned murals and sculpture for installation in the terminal buildings. The end result represented not only a response to earlier complaints about Canada's terminals, but also the creation of a new type of interior public space, one that was no longer related to a particular city but instead reflected the national culture through the combination of fine art, modernist architecture, and elegant furnishings.

The construction of these buildings coincided with what British architect and critic Deyan Sudjic has described as the

[b]aroque phase of airport construction, characterized by the outward show of luxury ... This was the modern world in its *Dolce Vita* incarnation: Cuban heels, Dacron, midnight-blue suits, and silver metal aircraft waiting to whisk the masters of the universe away ... In the dowdy London of the fifties, there was nothing that was quite so thoroughly modern as Heathrow. It was a place to escape from the messy world outside and bask in the sleek gloss of its wide-open spaces, the sheen of costly materials, voluptuous modern furniture and carefully coordinated lower case typography.[5]

London's Heathrow, in look and layout, set a pattern for many airports of the era; it was also one of the airports most affected by the cycle of obsolescence and explosive growth characteristic of the sixties and seventies. This trend had been foreshadowed a generation earlier in 1930s Berlin. Templehoff Airport, one of the world's busiest terminals by 1936, was already embarking on a planning exercise to replace a terminal only ten years old with one that could accommodate thirty times the traffic.[6] The visionary terminal, only partially realized owing to the conflict of World War II, was intended to handle passenger loads until the year 2000, an impossible exercise that could not anticipate changes in aircraft, in technology, or in security.

Not only did Canada's terminal-building program begin during a second generation of terminal expansion worldwide, it also came on the heels of a milestone in Canadian cultural history, the publication of the Massey Report in 1951. The report's primary thrust – to encourage the government to "forge and project a Canadian culture"[7] – led to the creation of the Canada Council for the Arts and the National Library and catalyzed cultural production in Canada until the seventies. At the heart of the report was the promotion of a recognizable expression of "true Canadianism."[8] The sentiment appeared, likely with no conscious link to the Massey Report, in 1958, when the architects for the Gander terminal suggested that an area of the international waiting lounge might be an appropriate place for a mural.[9] A limited competition led to the commissioning of *Flight and Its Allegories*, a 2.75 m x 22 m mural by Regina-based painter Ken Lochhead, and *Welcoming Birds*, a bronze and aluminum sculpture by Ottawa's Art Price. Fine art pieces were commissioned for subsequent terminals, but the art program did not reach its zenith until new air terminals were built in Toronto, Winnipeg, and Edmonton, where twenty pieces of painting and sculpture were commissioned and installed.

The influence of the Massey Report on air-terminal construction is clearly apparent, and it could be argued that the airport art project is a tangible example of the goals of the Massey Commission, embodying many of the directives related to public art and architecture, as well as the suggestion that governments become model patrons of the arts. Indeed, the Department of Transport allocated one-half of one per cent of the total airport-improvement budget to art. Central to the exercise was a nationalist quest that saw modernist art and architecture being used to create an identity for the nation. "There was no catering to popular taste ... We were trying to achieve for Canada the most sophisticated image we possibly could. There was no regional favouritism. We felt that it would be a service to Canadian culture to expose a Vancouver artist in Edmonton, Montreal artists in Toronto, Toronto artists in Winnipeg" (Figure 1.1).[10]

The Department of Transport Air Services Branch, under Chief Architect W.A. (Alex) Ramsay, was credited with the furniture selection and interior design. The branch was set up to design many of the smaller terminals and to oversee the work of the consulting architects responsible for the larger terminals. John C. Parkin, the chairman of the National Design Council and architect for the Toronto terminal, and Stanley White, who was employed by the Air Services Branch and was secretary of the art committee and the person responsible for coordination, were two personalities who had a major influence on the overall design direction. Mr White, who graduated from the University of Toronto School of Architecture in 1949, was described as "an accomplished designer-director in the amateur theatre, who has provided much of the impetus for a vastly improved standard of design."[11] Indeed, the new interiors benefited not only from well-designed furniture, but also from innovative furniture arrangements that brought together in a coherent design statement the various elements of the architecture and the public art. The selection of furniture, for example, suggested an underlying agenda that was both complex and ambitious. There seems to have been a didactic effort to expose Canadians to good design and also to raise the standard of design among Canadian manufacturers.

The Department has insisted on using furniture of the highest standard from at home and abroad without compromising on buying Canadian furniture if it is second best. At the same time it has worked very closely with Canadian manufacturers, explaining

FIGURE 1.1

International waiting lounge at Gander International Airport, 1959, showing
Robin Bush's Prismasteel seating, Ken Lochhead's *Flight and Its Allegories*,
and Art Price's *Welcoming Birds*

COLLECTION OF THE CANADIAN ARCHITECTURAL ARCHIVES, UNIVERSITY OF CALGARY,
PANDA ASSOCIATES FONDS, 181A/84.02, IMAGE PAN 60740-102
PHOTO: HUGH ROBERTSON

and encouraging them to exert greater efforts to improve their designs. This attitude has brought some Canadian furniture to a level of excellence which does indeed compare favourably with the best available from other countries. In Toronto, as in Winnipeg and Edmonton, one is given a valuable opportunity to admire excellent Canadian and imported furniture.[12]

In some of the less-public areas, it seems that "style" won out over "true Canadianism," since many of the pieces in these spaces were designed by Europeans or Americans and have since achieved iconic status. The VIP lounge in Edmonton received "Egg" chairs designed by the Danish designer and architect Arne Jacobsen and manufactured by Fritz Hansen. These were arrayed around a table (also manufactured by Hansen) by another Danish designer, Poul Kjaerholm. The VIP lounge in Winnipeg received elegant leather sling chairs by American designers William Katavolos, Ross Littell, and Douglas Kelley. The same programmatic area in the Toronto terminal also received American designs, in this case by Charles and Ray Eames for manufacturer Herman Miller. A hierarchy, perhaps unintended, was introduced through the furniture selection, international designs being used in the private lounges and Canadian designs in the public areas.

Two innovative Canadian designs were developed for the Toronto terminal. For the departure concourse, where sculptures by Kazuo Nakamura, entitled *Galaxy Numbers 1* and *2*, were suspended from the ceiling, Stefan Siwinski designed an extremely elegant seating system for production by his company, Korina Designs (Figure 1.2). For the holding rooms and inspection services areas, Robin Bush Associates of Toronto designed a line of component seating dubbed "Lollipop" for Canadian Office and School Furniture (Figure 1.3). The departure rooms featured an earlier Robin Bush design called Prismasteel – a design used extensively by the Department of Transport, including in the international waiting room at Gander in Newfoundland.

In the Edmonton terminal's lounges and departure concourse, two extraordinary environments were created through the combination of architecture, art, and furniture (Figure 1.4). The public lounge was furnished with unique three-legged chairs designed by Court Noxon for his own company, Metalsmiths; in their arrangement on circular rugs, the chairs complemented a curved Dennis Burton mural. The departure lounges featured component seating designed by Montreal's Douglas Ball. In the ticketing concourse, the angular sofas designed

FIGURE 1.2

Departure concourse at the Toronto International Airport, 1964, showing
Stefan Siwinski's 100-1 seating and Kazuo Nakamura's *Galaxy*

COLLECTION OF THE CANADIAN MUSEUM OF CONTEMPORARY PHOTOGRAPHY, 64-248,
NATIONAL GALLERY OF CANADA, OTTAWA
PHOTO: CHRIS LUND

FIGURE 1.3

Robin Bush, Lollipop component seating group for Canadian Office and School Furniture, 1963 (steel tube and hardware, black vinyl upholstery, moulded plywood, and foam)

COLLECTION OF DESIGN EXCHANGE, GIFT OF TORONTO CITY CENTRE AIRPORT AND THE TORONTO HARBOUR COMMISSION, 996.7
PHOTO: HARRY FOSTER, CANADIAN MUSEUM OF CIVILIZATION

FIGURE 1.4

Departure concourse at Edmonton International Airport, 1964, with Jack Shadbolt's
The Bush Pilot in the Northern Sky and seating by Robin Bush

COLLECTION OF THE PROVINCIAL ARCHIVES OF ALBERTA, PA531/5

by Robin Bush for Canadian Office and School Furniture were upholstered in a magenta colour and arranged in a geometric pinwheel pattern, offering a counterpoint to the muted colours of the lobby and the icy blue and white abstraction of Jack Shadbolt's 5.5 m x 11 m homage to Canadian bush pilots.

Several international designs were manufactured under licence by Canadian firms. The furniture used in the public lounge at the Toronto terminal offers two such examples: the cubic lounge chairs on one side of the room were designed by Swiss designer Robert Haussmann and manufactured under licence by Swiss Design of Canada, while the tub chairs at the other end of the lounge were designed by the American designer Ward Bennett for Lehigh and manufactured under licence in Montreal by Ebena-LaSalle. This room and the choice of furniture represented a curious design concept, the two styles of chairs being used to designate male- and female-themed areas, separated by a double-sided Louis de Niverville mural mounted on a freestanding screen. The Haussmann chairs, blocky, angular, and in dark colours, represented the masculine side of the room, while the Bennett chairs, rounded, voluptuous, pale, and positioned next to the children's play area, represented the female side of the room. Correspondence between John Gallop, interior designer with John B. Parkin Associates, and Stanley White confirms the intentionality of the concept: "In the briefest way I discussed our meeting with Mr John C. Parkin, as it turns out his own thinking parallels ours incredibly ... Mr J.C. sees the main lounge as divided into three or four distinct areas: Masculine – black, brown Atlas chairs?; feminine looking into the Nursery – Lehigh chairs? ..."[13]

A startling series of glamorous interiors was the overall result in the nationalist atmosphere of the time. Abstract painting and sculpture and modernist architecture and design were employed to represent the national Canadian identity in the country's effort to follow the international trend of constructing luxurious airport terminals. The furniture chosen for the terminal interiors was integral to the realization of a "Dolce Vita" image and to the creation of a new type of interior public space.

The public reception was mixed, the artworks in particular attracting considerable criticism owing to their cost and abstract nature. The problem of public perception was compounded in 1966 with the controversy surrounding the installation of a Greg Curnoe mural at Montreal's Dorval Airport, an artwork commissioned in preparation for Expo 67.

By the time the Vancouver International Airport was completed in 1968, the art program was throttled back to include just four pieces (Guido Molinari and Bodo Pfeiffer were commissioned for paintings rather than murals; Robert Murray's *Cumbria* sculpture was purchased for the exterior; and Robert Weghsteen was commissioned to design a brick wall in the baggage-claim lobby) and the idea of a national identity was cracking in the face of regionalist forces. Correspondence to Jean Sutherland Boggs, director of the National Gallery, illustrates the emerging desire to project a regionalist image and is oddly prophetic of the recent installations of First Nations art at the Vancouver Airport: "The suggestion for totem poles may be considered too 'bourgeois' for you, but with your guidance, we would like to consider the other suggestions."[14] The "other suggestions" came from Harold J. Merilees of the Vancouver Chamber of Commerce and included instructing artists to reflect the history, ethnic background, and geography of British Columbia.

The furniture in Vancouver International Airport (Figure 1.5), including "Facet" chairs by J. and J. Brook for Contemporary Distribution, was perhaps used more successfully than in any of the other airports. The Vancouver interiors were less carefully staged, and the atmosphere of the spaces was thus less dependent on such details as the actual arrangement of the furniture. The introduction of wood accents and warmer colours also contributed to the terminal's casual atmosphere. Being casual – and therefore flexible – the Vancouver design was more likely than most others to endure the enormous changes that air travel would undergo in the next decade as a result of ever-increasing passenger numbers and security issues. The fragility of most airport interior designs was noted in a Department of Transport memo from 1961 that laid out a schedule of aesthetic inspections:

For years the Department has been criticized for the inadequacy and ugliness of our public areas and many improvisations have been implemented from pure necessity. With the advent of new terminals and other buildings it is now important to guard against additions, alterations or constructions in the public eye which will detract from the new buildings.[15]

The incredible growth in airline passenger traffic is illustrated by the demolition of Toronto's 1964 terminal on its fortieth birthday. It has been replaced by the beginnings of a $4.4-billion terminal expansion that over the next fifteen-

FIGURE 1.5

Departure concourse at Vancouver International Airport, 1968, with Facet seating
by J. and J. Brook

plus years will see all three existing terminals at Pearson Airport replaced. The new super-airport is expected to be able to handle 50 million passengers annually, approximately twice the 2002 number.[16] Expansion of a similar nature is taking place across the country, signalling another terminal-building frenzy. This time the individual airport buildings are privately owned, and their designs are being shaped by security concerns and ever-growing passenger flows. Both issues have their roots in the 1970s and have been accelerated by the effects of airline deregulation and the terrorist events of 11 September 2001. Much of the early glamour of the Jet Age has been lost in the process.

The era it ushered in promised to be suave and cultured – think about that the next time you're walking through security in your socks or standing in line at Pretzel Time. But if the Jet Age never fully delivered on that promise, that's not because it failed – it's because it succeeded too well, generating a public demand that has constantly outstripped the industry's capacity. It's also because travelers craved an unattainably romantic notion of what air travel could represent.[17]

The romantic notions and nationalist aspirations suggested by the early terminals have been supplanted by a scramble to pay for constantly expanding and changing terminals through the creation of revenue-generating retail areas that tempt and entertain an increasingly jaded traveller. The design concepts for these areas tend to reflect the unique aspects of an individual city rather than evoke a national identity. This regionalist expression is conveyed by colour, lighting, dioramas, and themed interiors, as well as by the counters and installations individually designed for each terminal. The manufactured seating systems, rather than playing a defining role in the design, are usually chosen on the basis of cost, comfort, and the ability to blend into the overall theme. This direction has resulted in many attractive and comfortable interiors, but it is an environment far removed from the time when "la Dolce Vita" met "true Canadianism."

2

"Instant World": Canada and Space-Age Design in the Sixties

RACHEL GOTLIEB

During the sixties, not only did Canada make significant contributions to the development of communication satellite technology through government programs, but it also led in communications theory, championed by none other than the internationally published media guru Marshall McLuhan. Reflecting this new preoccupation with the future, many of Canada's designers drew inspiration from the space race and directed their innovations towards the burgeoning youth market and Hollywood.

By the end of the decade and in the early seventies, disillusionment had set in. The space-age movement ultimately failed, breaking its promise to deliver the better world of the future.[1]

Space-Age Satellites and Government Policies

In the sixties, Canada was at the forefront of satellite communications. This was due in part to our huge geographical area. Canada became a world leader in public broadcasting and telecommunications out of necessity. Alexander Graham Bell made his first long-distance telephone call in Canada in 1876; another Canadian, Reginald Fessenden, made the first live radio broadcast in 1906; and entrepreneur Edward (Ted) Rogers created the first alternating current (AC) tube in 1925, an invention that popularized the radio. In 1936 Parliament created the Canadian Broadcasting Corporation (CBC) to unite our vast and sparsely populated nation. By the late 1950s, the country was operating the largest television microwave network system in the world to service the needs of the CBC, which ran stations from coast to coast.

Canada officially entered the space age when it launched the all-Canadian-made satellite, *Alouette 1* (Figure 2.1). It was the third nation in the world to accomplish such a feat, following the superpowers, the Soviet Union and the United States. *Alouette* studied the earth's upper atmosphere to help scientists understand Canada's northern lights and how they affected radio communications. The silver satellite introduced the high-tech feature of long, collapsible antennae that extended open once the satellite was in orbit. The *Alouette 1* stayed in orbit ten years longer than predicted. Its success led to the creation of ISIS (International Satellite for Ionosphere Studies), which in turn produced three more atmospheric satellites.[2]

A tremendous excitement about the potential capabilities of satellite communications swept the nation. The experts hoped that this new technology would have the same, if not greater, impact on society as the great railroad did in the nineteenth century and serve as an important nation-building tool.[3] Yet there was also a real concern that a foreign state's ability to broadcast live by a direct signal into a private home could threaten the country's cultural sovereignty. The federal government thus felt pressured to exert control over the new technology of direct broadcast.[4] (In point of fact, direct-to-home satellite services occurred much later than anticipated and are still highly regulated. Only today are satellite dishes becoming commonplace, and even now they require a licensed intermediary.)

In the sixties, Canadian officials worked with the United Nations on co-drafting a law proclaiming that no country could beam a satellite signal into another country without the other country's consent. The government also introduced a number of important initiatives based on the recommendations of Dr John Chapman, the scientist who founded the Canadian satellite program. Heeding Chapman's advice, the government began to develop satellites for telecommunication rather than scientific purposes. It established the crown corporation Telesat Canada to build them and their required infrastructure of over one hundred ground receiving stations.[5] Also created was the Department of Communications (DOC) in 1968 to develop and direct policies based on these initiatives. The department intended to be a leader of research and development and

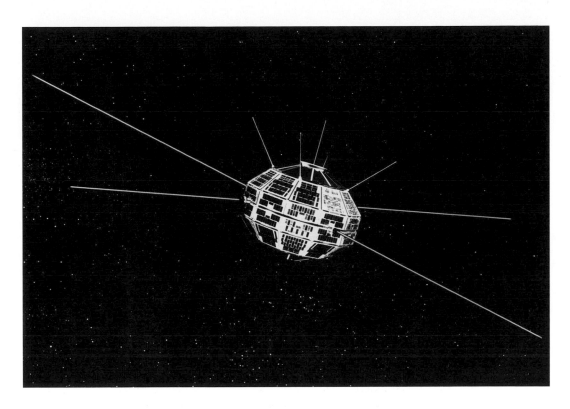

FIGURE 2.1

Artist's rendering of *Alouette 1*, launched by the Canadian Defence and Research
Telecommunications Establishment, 1962

not simply a regulatory board. One of its first tasks was to conduct the Telecommission, a comprehensive investigation into our changing world.[6]

The *Anik A1* satellite that was launched in orbit in 1972 was a manifestation of all these federally sponsored efforts. The Telecommission even ran a national open competition to find a name for the satellite. Such luminaries as Leonard Cohen and Marshall McLuhan formed part of the jury, and the committee chose from the list of entries the name *Anik*, which means brother in Inuit. This was an appropriate choice given that one of the purposes of the satellite was to beam telecommunications to the isolated Arctic. When Canada launched *Anik* into orbit, it became the first country in the world to have a non-military commercial geostationary telecommunication system. Used for telephone and television broadcasting, *Anik* linked the nation from coast to coast and, significantly, to the Arctic. The CBC became the first television station in the world to broadcast programs from a satellite. *Anik*'s more powerful successor, *Hermes*, launched in 1976, led to the development of direct-to-home satellite services, which were introduced in Canada in 1997.

Satellites, Stereos, and Sex Appeal

The federal government never created a program that would have involved sharing the results of space-age research with Canadian designers. There was no need because, fortunately for Canada and the rest of the world, Marshall McLuhan, the high priest of pop teaching at the University of Toronto, created the cultural atmosphere necessary for the digestion of these remarkable changes. He once stated, "Our world is mostly directed by groggy bureaucrats who decide to make innovations, such as satellite environments without thinking as to the social and psychological consequence."[7] It was left to McLuhan to translate it all into elliptical slogans, the most famous being "the global village" and "The medium is the message." McLuhan predicted that satellite communications would create an instant world. He inspired the free-spirited, sexually active youth, advised Prime Minister Trudeau, and consulted with blue chip American corporations. He became a media darling celebrated in films and magazines, giving *Playboy* an extensive interview in 1967.

If the high priest's teachings weren't enough, then there was the space race itself. From the 1957 launch of the *Sputnik* satellite by the Soviets to the *Apollo 11* moon landing of 1969, futuristic gadgetry and miniature technologies became the stuff of inspiration for designers. Space-age technology offered optimism and hope during the Cold War era. Designers raided all kinds of space-race products and gizmos for ideas – spacesuits, spaceships, space helmets, control labs, and aluminum satellites.

The new consumer electronics company Clairtone Sound Corporation in Rexdale, Ontario, became one of the first companies to successfully draw inspiration from the space age. At the time, Canada was not known as a leader in forward-thinking product design, but that changed with Clairtone's Project G stereo, launched in 1963 (Figure 2.2). The designer, Hugh Spencer, introduced twin gleaming, over-sized (47 cm), spun-aluminum-sphere speakers that clearly suggested satellite imagery. *Time* magazine featured the design and commented that the "unit comes not from Mars but from Canada."[8] The innovative design – the speakers extend outside the cabinet, making it the first to "break the box" – won a silver medal at Italy's prestigious international design fair, the Triennale di Milano, in 1964.

Space-age design is closely tied to the pop movement. Pop is about the fusion of popular culture, art, design, and fashion.[9] Clairtone developed a high-profile marketing campaign for Project G and the spin-off G2 and G3 stereos by making the most of popular culture. The company secured product endorsements from Hollywood stars – Frank Sinatra, Tuesday Weld, and Sonny and Cher, to name a few. It also saw its products placed in such stylish films as *A Fine Madness* (1966) and *The Graduate* (1967). In the former, Sean Connery plays a failed poet who works in a menial position at a corporate office that develops satellites. Is it any surprise that one scene shows him making out with a beautiful woman under a model of a satellite and next to the futuristic G2 stereo? Clairtone's globe speakers reflect the spirit of the day – both the space age and the sixties sexual revolution.

The initial success of Clairtone convinced Electrohome, an older and more conservative electronics company based in Kitchener, to change its ways and become more competitive. Rather than exploiting space-age design as an expression of fetish and desire, Electrohome emulated the Canadian government's new satellite communication strategy for our changing world. Electrohome's design director, Gordon Duern, served as the principal creative mind behind the new policy to develop products that would predict advances ten years into the future. For the Hemisphere '80, a visionary communications

FIGURE 2.2

Hugh Spencer, Project G stereo for Clairtone Sound Corporation, 1963 (Brazilian
Palisander [rosewood], leather, black anodized aluminum, brushed aluminum)

COLLECTION OF DESIGN EXCHANGE, GIFT OF PETER MUNK, 998.9
PHOTO: HARRY FOSTER, CANADIAN MUSEUM OF CIVILIZATION

system for the home, he proposed a lunar module suspended from the ceiling on a telescoping rod and operated by a wireless remote (Figure 2.3). The "rotating eye" would contain TV projection equipment and speakers to accompany the highly anticipated direct broadcast signal. The Hemisphere '80 was the last of Duern's visionary concepts for Electrohome. Unfortunately, the visionary design was purely conceptual and never made it past the drawing board.

However, for the Circa 75 stereo, Duern took the avant-garde design to actual prototype. The stereo featured a massive circular wooden console with circuitry board and accompanying wall-screen TV, as well as a cockpit chair with control buttons on the arms and speakers in the wings. The gadgets and even the language in the marketing materials reflected the new communications age.[10] Brochures proclaimed "[a] revolution in the making" with simultaneous linkups to "London ... the New York Stock Exchange ... a stadium in Moscow ... your local university and favourite stores."[11] A Design Canada report describes the Circa 75 as a daring research prototype that was intended to be a "communications nerve centre for the future."[12] This language echoes a description of the DOC, "the nerve system of the nation in search of itself."[13]

As with the Project G stereo, the visionary Circa 75 became the company's futuristic mascot. Electrohome produced a colour "infomercial" for the prototype and toured the design across the country, including to Montreal's Habitat during Expo 67. The excitement that surrounded Circa 75 inspired the company to develop the Circa Product Group. This included the Circa 703, a smaller and less advanced version that nevertheless still featured the cockpit-style sound chair to satisfy Electrohome's motto "the future today" (Figure 2.4). Electrohome made its Circa stereos with space-age materials to enhance the futurist styling, and no material more than plastic articulated the space-age look. Whether transparent, silver, or glossy white, it symbolized the material of the future and pervaded fashion, product design, and furniture.

In Canada, designers favoured acrylic to express the space-age look. Gordon Duern and junior designer Keith McQuarrie designed Apollo 860 for Electrohome as part of the previously mentioned Circa Product Group (Figure 2.5). Its name's allusion to the U.S. space program, its satellite ball speakers, and, most dramatically, its smoked acrylic bubble lid exemplified futurism. According to the Design Canada report, the company wanted to create a dynamic image to appeal to the growing teenage market. With this collection, Electrohome decided to follow Clairtone's lead and evoke the "Swinging Sixties" by

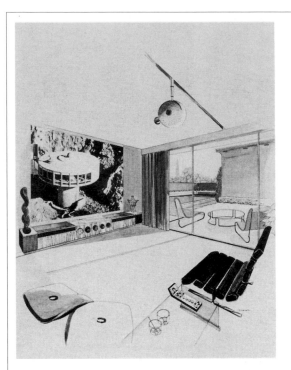 

IN THE FUTURE

Electrohome firmly believes in looking to tomorrow to give its customers the best today. That's why we introduced Circa '75 – the communications nerve center of the future which encompassed all elements of audio visual equipment, including wall screen TV, video monitor and home shopping.

Based on the concept of Circa '75 has come an ultra modern line of stereo units that has received wide spread recognition throughout the world, both for its styling and performance.

And now Electrohome introduces a new concept – Hemisphere '80 – our latest look into communications of tomorrow that is bound to add to our growing list of industry firsts.

FIGURE 2.3

Gordon Duern, Hemisphere '80 for Electrohome Ltd, 1971

*T*HE FUTURE NOW

The Electrohome Circa 703 and Sound Chair is a complete break with everything traditional. It is "the future . . . today".
The Circa 703, a suspended form, is perfectly round to make it timeless in design, now, you can have a music center, AM/FM FM Stereo, which is the local point of the room and is compatible with many more styles of homes and furniture. The total environment chair or sound chair is truly a step into the future. The black egg shell form with gleaming spider base is a perfect companion for your Circa 703 Stereo. The chair will adjust to your comfort and in finger tip reach is your multi-function control panel which allows you to tune automatically and adjust your volume. Delicately balanced stereo speakers are at ear-level, carrying you into the world of tomorrow . . . today.

FIGURE 2.4

Gordon Duern, Circa 703 for Electrohome Ltd, 1967

FIGURE 2.5

Gordon Duern and Keith McQuarrie, Apollo 860 for Electrohome Ltd, 1966
(Plexiglas, brushed aluminum)

COLLECTION OF CANADIAN MUSEUM OF CIVILIZATION, 2004.7.1
PHOTO: HARRY FOSTER, CANADIAN MUSEUM OF CIVILIZATION

highlighting the products as objects of desire. The brochure boasted that the flying saucer Apollo was "designed for the now generation" and, to emphasize the design's erotic appeal, included a young, barefoot model in a psychedelic pantsuit beside the product.

Demise

As Marshall McLuhan observed, "if it works, then it's obsolete." The problem with technology is that it becomes out of date once it enters the marketplace. Space-age design eventually became too familiar and fell out of fashion. Even the groundbreaking Clairtone Sound Corporation suffered a spectacular fall and eventually went bankrupt. The youth movement matured and realized that the billions required to finance the necessary research and development for the space race meant less funding for other rising concerns, notably the environment and world peace.

Society's disillusionment with the space race was played out on the Hollywood screen. The plot of *Diamonds Are Forever* (1971) centres on a communications satellite powered by diamonds. The master criminal, Blofeld, transforms the emancipating tool of the global village into an earth-scorching weapon of mass destruction.

Only now, at the dawn of the new century, are we seeing a renewed interest in futurist design. Witness the countless reissues of space-age sixties products on the one hand and radical out-of-this-world architecture populating our urban centres on the other. Is it nostalgia for the past or the anticipation of tomorrow that fuels this new futurism?

3

A Flag for Canada

MICHAEL LARGE

In 1964 Lester B. Pearson, Canada's fourteenth prime minister, spoke of the country's need for its own national symbol:

I believe most sincerely that it is now time for Canadians to unfurl a flag that is truly distinctive and truly national in character; as Canadian as the maple leaf which should be its dominant design, a flag easily identifiable as Canada's; a flag which cannot be mistaken for the emblem of any other country; a flag of the future which honours also the past; Canada's own and only Canada's.[1]

The maple leaf flag is the most nationally significant (and destined to be the most durable) Canadian design artifact from the sixties. Canada had previously used the Red Ensign, featuring the British Union Jack and the arms granted by King George V in 1921 (Figure 3.1). The arms, which had been modified and legally protected in the 1950s, were the only part of the flag to distinguish the Red Ensign of Canada from that of several other Commonwealth countries. Canada still does not have the panoply of national symbolism of older countries such as the United States, but its government had far less visual impact before the sixties. The contrast between the beginning and end of the decade is stark, particularly if we see the flag as part of the systematized use of visual symbols of nationhood; more change of a symbolic nature occurred in a few years than in the whole of Canadian history.

Proposals to change the flag had been made many times before, so why did the idea take hold so firmly and become a reality so rapidly? Arguments about aesthetics and traditions took place against a backdrop of widely experienced sixties phenomena (social revolution, the coming of age of the baby boomers, a long economic boom) and the specifically Canadian issues of national unity, language, and identity. In the emotional debates about the flag in 1964, Prime Minister Pearson made it clear that one of the most pressing concerns of the Liberal government was the threat to the unity of the country posed by the growth of the Quebec separatist movement.[2]

Organizations of all kinds, including nations, change their symbols to reflect new realities. Historian Eric Hobsbawm has commented on the importance of "the invention of emotionally and symbolically charged signs of club membership ... highly relevant to that comparatively recent historical innovation, the 'nation,' with its associated phenomena: nationalism, the nation-state, national symbols, histories and the rest."[3] In the sixties, the government of Canada's review of its entire communications structure was a logical response to circumstance. The government needed to be seen, and seen as legitimate, in a country that was being transformed. Forty years later, it can be said not only that the flag succeeded in breaking with the past and establishing a new presence for Canada, but that it was also prescient in announcing what the country was becoming.

Design in the Sixties

It was fitting that a reinvention of the national image should have been undertaken in the sixties. In every Western country, technological and economic optimism, social revolution, and a burgeoning youth culture made everything seem possible. The decade marked the last time that design could confidently celebrate modernity without reservation or irony.

The start of the decade marked the high tide of the international style, the postwar version of modernism that believed in rational design solutions and the perfection of form and systems. However, it was also in the sixties that modernism was overwhelmed by the energy of popular culture. The decade marked what historian Philippe Garner has termed "the triumph of the

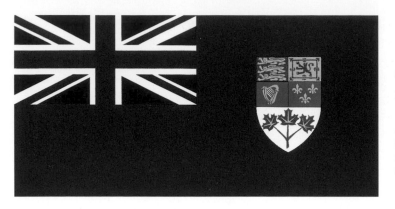

FIGURE 3.1

Red Ensign

COURTESY OF THE
DEPARTMENT OF CANADIAN
HERITAGE, GOVERNMENT
OF CANADA

consumer, particularly the young consumer, the idea of style and design impos-ing themselves from the street up."[4] In this environment, the power of the designer was, as critic Reyner Banham remarked in his 1955 essay "A Throw-Away Aesthetic" (first published in 1960), "his command and understanding of popular symbolism."[5] This is particularly true of communications design. Our crowded image landscape really started to take shape in the sixties, the decade that saw television, advertising, and the corporate visual presence begin to dominate the environment as never before, giving designers a central role in the development of visual culture and prompting Marshall McLuhan's astute commentary in his groundbreaking *Understanding Media* (1964).

Both modernist and participatory, popular culture trends were strongly influ-ential in Canada. The international style in graphic design, exhibiting a purist approach to layout and typography, emanated from Switzerland and was widely adopted, especially in government and corporate work. The Swiss typeface Helvetica, an icon of the international style, would be chosen at the end of the decade for Canadian government communications. The European influence was brought here by immigrants such as Rolf Harder and Ernst Roch and by returning Canadians, notably Paul Arthur, who had worked at *Graphis* magazine in Switzerland. Arthur became the managing editor of *Canadian Art*, and his design projects included signage for Canadian airports and the graphics for Expo 67. Graphics had been at the forefront of Canadian visual culture since the time of the Group of Seven (several of whom had careers in design and illustration), and in the sixties a brilliant group of young designers emerged, acutely aware of international trends. Many had worked on major corporate identity programs for design firms such as Stewart and Morrison in Toronto, demonstrating their ability to create both design systems and memorable logos for large organizations, perhaps the most famous example of the latter being the logo for Canadian National drawn by Allan Fleming in 1959.[6]

Designing the Flag

Modernist principles were evident in the development of the flag, both in the newly centralized direction and systematic deployment of visual identity in government communications and in the meticulous attention to technical standards. A genuinely populist involvement was also demonstrated in the passion of the public debate and the extraordinary range of flag proposals submitted by Canadians. The question of a new flag had been raised repeatedly since World War II, and in 1963 *Canadian Art* and *Perspectives/Weekend Magazine* jointly organized a competition that drew 789 entries, many from prominent designers such as Allan Fleming, Ernst Roch, Rolf Harder, and the typographic designer Carl Dair. The winners were published in the September/October edition of *Canadian Art* under the title "In Search of Meaningful Canadian Symbols." The editorial stated, "Every society, like every individual person, needs a sense of identity – the sense of being individual and different."[7] The winners, however, reflected modernist abstraction more than individual expressiveness. The overall winning design, by Montreal designer Rolland Lavoie, resembled the Japanese flag but with the disc half red and half blue (Figure 3.2). Allan Fleming's design consisted of overlapping yellow and blue circles on a white ground, and other designs featured arrangements of circles representing the provinces (Figure 3.3). Several winning entries did acknowledge popular symbolism by incorporating highly stylized versions of the maple leaf.

The three judges were Dr Geoffrey C. Andrew, executive director, Canadian Universities Foundation, Ottawa; Ted Bethune, creative director, Cockfield, Brown Ltd, Vancouver; and Guy Viau, critic and vice-president of the Arts Council of Quebec, Montreal. Commenting on the issues, Andrew said, "We are trying to do something that is really difficult and which has, in fact, never been

FIGURE 3.2

Rolland Lavoie's winning entry in *Canadian Art* and *Perspectives/Weekend Magazine*'s
flag competition, 1963

CANADIAN ART, SEPTEMBER/OCTOBER 1963

FIGURE 3.3

Allan R. Fleming's submission to *Canadian Art* and *Perspectives*/*Weekend Magazine*'s
flag competition, 1963

CANADIAN ART, SEPTEMBER/OCTOBER 1963
COPYRIGHT ALLAN R. FLEMING, FGDC, FRCA, AGI, FOCA
COURTESY OF THE FLEMING ESTATE

done before – to blend two languages and many cultures in one viable national identity." Bethune added, "What *really* stood out was that the citizens of Canada whether of French origin, English origin, or whatever, newcomers and fourth generation people alike, were striving to create a *new* symbolism." The context for this exercise was an increasingly confrontational political situation. The year of the competition also saw the instigation of the Royal Commission on Bilingualism and Biculturalism, which would work for six years on a series of reports, resulting in the Official Languages Act of 1969. The year 1963 also marked the founding of the FLQ (Front de libération du Québec), whose activities were to culminate in the October Crisis of 1970 and the invocation of the War Measures Act. As Canada approached the centenary of Confederation, there was a strong desire for a new Canadian flag that would transcend divisive history and symbolize a united, multicultural identity.

The eventual selection process employed by the government in 1964 was lengthy and strenuously contested, demonstrating the power of visual symbols to arouse emotions. After an acrimonious series of debates in the House of Commons (the Opposition was led by a resolute John Diefenbaker), the matter was referred to an all-party committee of fifteen members of Parliament. The thousands of designs submitted, by amateurs and by professional artists and designers, reflected the issues at the heart of the debate and a recognition of the opportunity to shape a new visual identity for the nation.

The designs may be grouped in three categories: traditional, emphasizing links with Britain and France; representational, employing established icons such as beavers and maple leafs; and abstract (stripes, stars, or circles). Many of the designs inspired by tradition tended to be awkward combinations of fleurs-de-lys and Union Jacks, elements that do not sit well together graphically. The representational designs, in trying to be inclusive, were also cluttered. The maple leaf was the most common illustrative emblem, though often so strangely rendered as to be almost unrecognizable, and the leaf did not lend itself well to repetition in rows like the stars on the American flag. Painter A.Y. Jackson proposed several designs, one using the three-leaf, heraldic form of the maple from the arms, another a single leaf (Figure 3.4).

Ultimately, the committee reduced the submissions to fifteen finalists in three groups: the three-leaf designs, single-leaf designs, and those employing references to Britain and France. After six weeks of meetings and secret ballots, the three finalists, one from each group, were announced. One was the three-

FIGURE 3.4

A.Y. Jackson's submission to the Flag Committee, 1964

leaf emblem in red on a white ground, with blue bars (favoured by Pearson), another was the eventual flag but with a thirteen-point maple leaf, and the third was the same, but with the addition of the Union Jack and the fleur-de-lys. George Stanley, dean of arts at the Royal Military College, had first sketched the winning design. It was redrawn and simplified to an eleven-point design by Jacques Saint-Cyr, a designer working for the federal government, and approved by the prime minister on 9 November 1964. The chosen flag then faced a Tory filibuster in Parliament before being proclaimed on 28 January 1965.[8]

The Visible World

The new flag emphasized continuity (by using the maple leaf and Canada's traditional colours of red and white) and distinctiveness (by dropping the visual reference to Britain). Its recognition was reinforced by consistent implementation, demonstrating the core cultural aims of all visual-identity programs. In his memoir, flag committee member John Ross Matheson recounts how the committee took extraordinary care to select the best red and choose the perfect fabric, making use of the latest research and technical expertise. The Canadian Specifications Board issued a directive with minutely detailed specifications.[9]

By the second half of the sixties, the government's determination to overcome political and linguistic disunity, combined with Canada's growing design expertise, made possible a remarkably systematized, sophisticated approach to national identity. After the flag was proclaimed in 1965, the eleven-point maple leaf was legally protected, and the logo that was to be adopted as the "Canada" wordmark was created at McLaren Advertising for the Canadian Government Travel Bureau. This was followed by the proclamation of the Official Languages Act in 1969, the issuing of the report of the Task Force on Government Information in the same year, and the establishment in 1970 of Information Canada, which was to oversee all government communications, including the Federal Identity Program (Figure 3.5). The latter – one of the largest such programs in the world – controlled all government nomenclature, use of symbols, and even signage. Significantly, the founding of Information Canada was a response to recommendations in a government report called "To Know and Be Known." Visibility was the key, for government as for large corporations. The aims of the program were to promote recognition of, and access to, government services,

Canada

FIGURE 3.5

The "Canada" Wordmark, Government of Canada, 1965

to project both official languages equally, to improve efficiency and savings in government communications, and to exploit design as a management tool. Although Information Canada was disbanded in 1976, the visual identity of the government has undergone no major changes since the 1980s. In a world where visual identities have ever-shorter life cycles, continuity has been a mark of the program's success.[10]

The flag and the consistent implementation of the federal identity have proved to be effective. Federal visibility has been amplified by the flag's enthusiastic adoption and adaptation by artists, corporations, advertisers, and individual citizens. The flag asserts the national identity in a federation in which several layers of government compete. The provinces also use design in promoting their presence, from the buffalo of Manitoba and the wheat sheaf of Saskatchewan to the trillium of Ontario and fleur-de-lys of Quebec. Illustrating the uneasy relationship between the past and the future, Ontario and Quebec, in their own identity programs, still use symbolism deriving from their respective founding nations in their flags.

The global media environment that emerged in the sixties is now so pervasive, with visual persuasion and manipulation filling every possible space, that many regard it as threatening. Canadians have always been astute commentators on the situation, from Marshall McLuhan with his vision of the global village to, more recently, Naomi Klein and the writers for the Vancouver magazine *Adbusters* with their cynical critiques.[11] However, in multicultural, rapidly changing environments, where assumptions made in more homogeneous, stable circumstances no longer hold, there is a need for cohesion expressed in recognizable symbols (for quality, authority, or stability). In the sixties, Canada's modern, post-colonial identity came into focus. The flag has succeeded because it has achieved widespread association with values that individual Canadian citizens hold dear, embodying the uniqueness and continuity of Canada.

canada welcomes the world

4

Excellence, Inventiveness, and Variety: *Canadian Fine Crafts* at Expo 67

SANDRA ALFOLDY

Moncrieff Williamson had a vision for Canadian crafts, which had long been considered to be the preserve of ethnographers and women's groups. The crafts exhibited at Expo 67, the Montreal World's Fair, would give a new impression of Canadian work – as contemporary, sophisticated, and hip. In his role as crafts selection commissioner general to the Canadian Government Pavilion at Expo 67, Williamson succeeded in producing what was possibly Canada's most influential craft exhibition, *Canadian Fine Crafts*. However, this story is as much an account of the struggle to find a permanent home for Canada's crafts, one that would highlight the contemporary innovations on display in Montreal, as it is about the undeniably important role of crafts at the World's Fair (Figure 4.1).

By the time Moncrieff Williamson was charged with the task of elevating Canadian crafts to international heights in the form of *Canadian Fine Crafts*, he occupied a prominent role in the Canadian cultural field. Born in Scotland in 1915 to an aristocratic family, Williamson was educated at the Edinburgh College of Art and in World War II undertook secret Foreign Office assignments in Europe.[1] In 1957 he moved to Canada, where he was a curator at the Extension Services of the Art Gallery of Victoria before becoming the director of the art department at the Glenbow Foundation in Calgary in 1960. In 1964 Williamson took on the prestigious position as the first director of the new Confederation Centre Art Gallery in Charlottetown.[2] In his new directorship role, Williamson quickly adopted the position of art gallery revolutionary.[3]

FIGURE 4.1

Installation of *Canadian Fine Crafts* at the Canadian Government Pavilion,
Montreal World's Fair, 1967

COLLECTION OF LIBRARY AND ARCHIVES CANADA, PA-212926

At the 1965 Canadian Conference of the Arts held in Ste Adele, Quebec, Williamson gave a bold presentation, "The New Museums and Art Galleries: 1967 and After." It is apparent from this paper that he took an interdisciplinary approach to the arts and fully expected that fine crafts would occupy an equal position alongside Canada's other forms of artistic production.[4] In 1965 Williamson participated in the founding meeting of the Canadian Craftsmen's Association in Winnipeg, "a highly professional group, embracing all that is visual."[5] His own revolutionary views on art may well have been expanded through the association's emphasis on the environmental arts. Craftspeople were urged to embrace more than simply crafts – to consider, for example, prototypes for industrial production. Indeed, seven of the craftspeople participating in the Winnipeg conference later had their work exhibited as part of *Canadian Fine Crafts*.[6] From 1965 on, Williamson was considered a key figure for craftspeople, a man of influence in Canadian culture who supported craft. It is important to note, however, that Williamson was receptive to a particular type of craft. With his friend Norah McCullough, the founder of the Canadian Craftsmen's Association and western liaison officer of the National Gallery of Canada, Williamson shared the view that "excellence, inventiveness, [and] variety" defined the best of contemporary Canadian craft.[7]

McCullough and Williamson had more in common than simply an interest in the crafts; both were curating exhibitions titled *Canadian Fine Crafts* for Canada's centennial celebrations, McCullough's to be held at the National Gallery of Canada. Rather than competing with each other to secure Canada's top contemporary craftspeople, they decided to collaborate. In the summer of 1965, McCullough visited Williamson in Charlottetown for two days, where they "had very thorough discussions regarding not only the Expo Crafts Exhibition, but the National Gallery Exhibition as well."[8] McCullough made it clear to Williamson that she had a particular agenda in mind for her exhibition: "I will report to you what I strongly recommend. My guiding slogan is broad coverage (in order to defeat pedantive [sic] judgments, and also those who think of craftsmen as mere hobbyists) ... This should make it possible to include anything from a wooden scoop to a Cavelti jewel."[9] While Williamson may have been appreciative of non-traditional craft, he was very aware that in his role as crafts selection commissioner general to the Canadian Government Pavilion he had an obligation to provide a representative cross-section of the variety of crafts being produced in Canada. Nonetheless, while *Canadian Fine Crafts* presented both traditional and contemporary approaches to craft, the biographical backgrounds of the artists and consultants involved indicate that the contributors to the show were a group of like-minded professionals who supported more conceptual work.

Over 75 per cent of the 120 exhibitors had received professional training, with many of the craftspeople complementing their Canadian education with art school or apprenticeship in the United States and Europe.[10] Williamson's catalogue essay for *Canadian Fine Crafts* was carefully inclusive, acknowledging the influence of France on the advanced contemporary standards of Quebec's craft training as well as the "mosaic of imported European styles" so important throughout Canada. In an effort to avoid creating inequality between the urban and rural participants, he noted the role of rural craftspeople as equal to that of the professionals operating in the urban centres. Despite this balance, certain craftspeople emerged from *Canadian Fine Crafts* as outstanding. Mariette Rousseau-Vermette had two wool tapestries in the exhibition, *Brazero* and *Dawn or Night*, the latter purchased by Williamson for the Confederation Centre Art Gallery. Rich in texture and colour, and often monumental in scale, Rousseau-Vermette's tapestries were well known by the time of Expo 67, as she had achieved fame in the craft world when she was commissioned to create a curtain for the Eisenhauer Theater in Washington as a gift from the Canadian government.[11] André Malraux, France's minister of cultural affairs, singled out Rousseau-Vermette's work at *Canadian Fine Crafts* for special comment, further cementing her international status (Figure 4.2).[12] Embarrassingly, Rousseau-Vermette had difficulty finding her piece *Brazero* when she visited the exhibition, an indication of the architectural difficulties inherent in hosting an interdisciplinary display within the constrained space of the Canadian pavilion.

Initially, crafts had not been considered a necessary part of the gallery displays at the pavilion. While painting and sculpture were absolutes, the Fine Arts Advisory Committee of the Canadian Government Committee, 1967 Exhibition, was less certain of crafts, commenting in 1964, "It was agreed also that discussion of possible exhibits of graphics, photographs, architecture, and ceramics, enamels, tapestries, etc, should be postponed until the architects had had an opportunity to see what further space could be provided for them."[13] In the end, Williamson was given in the neighbourhood of a thousand square feet to exhibit Canadian crafts, a tiny space for a large task. Despite the small area, the architects working on the Canadian pavilion provided unique solutions for display, designing "six octagonal display cases built of rough deeply burnt brick

FIGURE 4.2

Mariette Rousseau-Vermette, *Dawn or Night*, 1966–67 (wool tapestry)

and lighted from within" and "a series of brick terraces ... as an area for pottery and possibly fabrics or larger objects." Out of necessity, some tapestries had to be displayed high above the display cases, therefore appearing lost, as in the case of Rousseau-Vermette's *Brazero*.[14]

Despite the spatial restrictions, objects were effectively displayed at *Canadian Fine Crafts*. More importantly, the fact that the shared gallery space of the Canadian pavilion highlighted crafts alongside paintings, graphics, sculpture, photography, and architecture prompted some critics to acknowledge that crafts were of "sufficiently high quality to rank as art."[15] Several of the works Williamson selected for the exhibition were playful objects, particularly the pieces in textile. The cover of the *Canadian Fine Crafts* catalogue featured Heather Maxey's *Florigorm*, a colourful combination of cloth collage and appliqué with stitchery (Figure 4.3). Maxey's piece echoes the biomorphic modernism of the time, featuring organic radiating shapes in a geometric pattern that surround what appears to be a colourful and densely patterned tree of life. Bright greens and reds share the tapestry's surface with the impressive needlework that betrays Maxey's training in stitchery and ecclesiastical embroidery in England.

Canadian Fine Crafts highlighted a diverse array of textile works and an exciting combination of approaches to metal and stained glass. What is striking, however, is that almost all the ceramic objects were stoneware. Williamson addressed this in his essay, writing, "In ceramics perhaps the common denominator is the marked use of stoneware from coast to coast and the warm earth colours associated with such products."[16] Although he sought inclusiveness, Williamson praised particular craftspeople for their ability to shift away from function. In this group, he included Nova Scotia's Charlotte Lindgren, whose wool and lead wire hanging *Winter Tree* was installed as sculpture, and Alberta's Ed Drahanchuk, whose pottery forms, although frequently functional, operated as free-standing sculpture. Drahanchuk's ceramic floor vase, listed by Williamson in the catalogue as "One Large Ceramic Floor Vase," stands an impressive 63.5 cm in height and achieves a diameter of 40.6 cm (Figure 4.4). It is finished in a rough brown glaze, with thick impasto surface decoration. Although Drahanchuk's stoneware pieces are organic and relatively coarse in their surface treatment, in no way were they considered outside the dominant aesthetic of the time. Indeed, Drahanchuk's work was featured in the interiors of Moshe Safdie's Habitat.

FIGURE 4.3

Heather Maxey, *Florigorm*, 1966–67 (appliqué wall hanging)

COLLECTION OF THE CONFEDERATION CENTRE OF THE ARTS, CHARLOTTETOWN, CM 67.1.39

PHOTO: CAMERA ART — CHARLOTTETOWN

COURTESY OF HEATHER MAXEY

FIGURE 4.4

Ed Drahanchuk, floor vase, 1966–67 (stoneware)

COLLECTION OF THE
CONFEDERATION CENTRE OF
THE ARTS, CHARLOTTETOWN,
CM 67.1.13

PHOTO: CAMERA ART –
CHARLOTTETOWN

COURTESY OF
ED DRAHANCHUK

Mariette Rousseau-Vermette's *Dawn or Night*, Heather Maxey's *Florigorm*, Charlotte Lindgren's *Winter Tree*, and Ed Drahanchuk's ceramic floor vase were some of the sixty-nine objects exhibited at *Canadian Fine Crafts* purchased by Williamson for the Confederation Centre. As early as 1965, Williamson made public his intention to create a gallery for contemporary crafts.[17] Inspired by the Canadian Craftsmen's Association and Expo 67's interdisciplinary visions for the arts, Williamson began actively purchasing crafts for the centre's art gallery, spending $10,000 on works from *Canadian Fine Crafts*.[18]

Prior to his involvement in Expo 67, Williamson had been a committed member of the Canadian Museums Association, and through that organization he had been made aware that there was no national museum for the crafts. This is not to say that collections of Canadian craft had not been previously formed. Sandra Flood has discussed in detail the assembling of craft in Canada up to 1950, concluding that thirteen collections were established between 1908 and 1937.[19] Interestingly, Flood discovered that the federal Interdepartmental Committee on Canadian Handicrafts (a short-lived body set up by the Department of Agriculture that existed from 1942 to 1944) recommended that the National Gallery of Canada encourage crafts because, according to their official report, "[a]rt institutions, whether in Europe or North America, which have adopted the policy of displaying and encouraging the creative hand arts and crafts, have observed a rapid increase in the numbers of people who visit such institutions as compared with the numbers who visit art services offering only fine paintings and sculpture."[20] The Canadian Handicrafts Guild's permanent collection, comprised largely of traditional and indigenous craft, and housed on Peel Street in Montreal was the most comprehensive permanent collection of crafts in Canada. Pieces from the collection were used as educational tools and were often borrowed for international exhibitions.[21]

Williamson believed that as a result of technological advances, it was now possible for a craftsperson in Prince Edward Island to produce "objects up to the required standard to market them in any part of the world."[22] Therefore, establishing a national craft museum in Charlottetown was a perfectly feasible idea, and Williamson envisioned this museum expanding, "[e]ventually to take over the present legislative building, transforming the present offices into period rooms relating to Island and Confederation history … In addition he forsees the establishment of craft study collections, didactic displays and a craft library, and the encouragement of active summer workshops."[23] He enthusiastically promoted his idea, and his purchase of objects from *Canadian Fine Crafts* was symbolic of the beginning of a national collection of contemporary craft. In his letters to the craftspeople whose Expo 67 pieces he had purchased, Williamson wrote that it was his intention to include their work in "our developing crafts museum."

Sadly, his vision was never realized, perhaps because of the post-Expo economic realities faced by the cultural sector. According to the Canadian Conference of the Arts, a pre-Expo level of cultural funding would only be acceptable to the arts community if the federal government undertook to support "not a twelve month but a three to five year program."[24] Perhaps Williamson himself developed a different vision for the role of crafts at the Confederation Centre. While new cases were built to display crafts at the centre, there were very few acquisitions after 1968, and eventually the pieces from Expo 67 were simply integrated into the collection.[25] While the project of a national craft museum may have been abandoned, Williamson remained involved in promoting the crafts, albeit on a smaller scale. Throughout the 1970s and early 1980s, the Confederation Centre Art Gallery hosted several exhibitions of crafts, including wall hangings by Wendy Toogood (1971) and ceramics by David Gilhooly (1979) and Robin Hopper (1980).

Despite the euphoria over the success of Canadian crafts at Expo 67 (Figure 4.5) and the continuing popularity of fine crafts, the 1970s were difficult years in terms of the establishment of a national museum for crafts. In addition to the loss of Williamson's plan for a national collection, the National Gallery of Canada did not host a large-scale exhibition of contemporary crafts in that decade, and in 1970 the permanent collection of the Canadian Guild of Crafts was devolved.[26] By 1982, however, the Canadian Crafts Council (an amalgamation of the Canadian Craftsmen's Association and the Canadian Handicrafts Guild) had picked up the cause of a national museum of crafts and design. Their proposal sounded remarkably similar in scope to Williamson's plan of nearly twenty years earlier, with a focus on contemporary work and craftspeople "in residence."[27]

In 1988 the Canadian Crafts Museum was opened in Vancouver, in large part the result of the success of the Cartwright Gallery on Granville Island. Tremendous excitement surrounded the establishment of Canada's first national institution devoted exclusively to the crafts. The mandate of the Canadian Crafts Museum was to preserve fine craft while demonstrating its social relevance, and it appeared that the museum's prominent location on Hornby

FIGURE 4.5

Installation of *Canadian Fine Crafts* at the Canadian Government Pavilion, Montreal World's Fair, 1967

Street, near the Vancouver Art Gallery, would ensure public interest. Sadly, despite a name change to the Canadian Craft and Design Museum in 2002, the under-funded museum was forced to close in that year. Ironically, while Moncrieff Williamson believed that technological advances would allow a national craft museum to survive in Charlottetown as early as 1965, on the opposite coast the Canadian Craft and Design Museum was unable to link Canada together over thirty years later.

In 1982, while the Canadian Crafts Council was putting forward its arguments for the creation of a national museum of crafts and design, two key events took place in the world of craft: Stephen Inglis was hired by the Canadian Museum of Civilization, and the Massey Foundation Collection of Crafts was gifted to the museum. Under the guidance of Inglis, the Museum of Civilization rethought its categorization of craft as ethnography or folklore, thus creating the opportunity for contemporary craft to be welcomed into its collection. In collaboration with the Canadian Crafts Council, the museum began collecting works by the winners of the Saidye Bronfman Award for Excellence in the Fine Crafts, established in 1977, and when the new Canadian Museum of Civilization building opened in 1989, the museum's craft collections, both historical and contemporary, were given proper storage conditions. With the hiring of Alan Elder in 2002 as Canada's first national curator of crafts and design, the Canadian Museum of Civilization reinforced its position as repository of Canada's pre-eminent craft collection.

Although Moncrieff Williamson's dream for a national craft museum never fully materialized and many of the objects that were exhibited at *Canadian Fine Crafts* now look "of that time," the message for Canadian crafts presented at Expo 67 remains as strong today as ever. In Williamson's words, "Canadian crafts have never been more in demand."[28]

5

Habitat '67: View from the Inside

PAUL BOURASSA

Surely no Canadian architectural project has ever received as much media attention as Habitat '67.[1] Moshe Safdie's design – an application of a three-dimensional modular building system – is mentioned in every history of contemporary architecture. Benefiting from the extraordinary showcase of Expo 67,
the Montreal World's Fair, Habitat '67 became one of the symbols of the
avant-garde at the event, the theme of which was "Man and His World." Safdie
attempted to put into practice the ideas he had put forward in a thesis he had
written at McGill University in 1960 concerning a "system of spatial urbaniza-
tion with unlimited growth potential, based on the three-dimensional network-
ing of elements that are standardized and can be fit together harmoniously to
fulfill all the urban functions in variable, complex, and evolving patterns."[2] The
final project, however, quickly became a "techno-village arranged in terraces on
the water's edge,"[3] and very few other projects were built using this system.

In terms of design, Moshe Safdie took particular interest in certain architectural details (handrails, walkways, lighting fixtures)[4] and in the functional rooms,
especially the kitchen and bathroom. From the outset, these rooms were conceived within the overall context of the project. In July 1965, Safdie talked about
a "modular kitchen," a single unit that was developed and constructed by Frigidaire and incorporated storage space, electrical appliances, and lighting.[5] In
June 1967, the 114 units of "Cuisine [Kitchen] 67," as it was then called, were
presented to the media in five different combinations and six colour schemes,
laid out in long narrow rooms in which the perspective was accentuated by the

Translated from the French by Phyllis Aronoff and Howard Scott

play of perpendicular lines (Figure 5.1).[6] The cupboards, refrigerator, and range, in plastic laminate with aluminum mouldings and no visible hardware, contributed to the purity of the whole look.[7] Several of the architect's sketches show the attention paid to formal balance in this experimental kitchen.

The bathroom also received special attention. In all, 282 units were produced in four different configurations. Walls, ceiling, floor, sink, counter, bathtub, and shower were all moulded out of fibreglass-reinforced plastic, another application of the idea of using prefabricated forms developed by architects for a given project. (Interestingly, the bathrooms were sponsored in part by Fiberglass Canada Ltd and Canadian Pittsburgh Industries.) For Safdie, a conventional bathroom would have ruined the modularity of the construction process, and he devoted himself to its design, playing an active role in the fabrication of the moulds at Reff Plastics in Toronto.[8] The magazine articles that sang his bathroom's praises (no finishing, easy to install and maintain, material less cold to the touch and less slippery)[9] used the same iconography that had described the housing modules, playing up the image of complete bathroom units hoisted by a crane, "ready to be dropped into position in one of the Habitat '67 housing units at Expo."[10]

A Series of Compromises

In addition to being an architectural experiment, Habitat was a theme pavilion at Expo 67, open to the public. It presented a vision of urban housing that was a key element in the neighbouring pavilion, "Man in the Community." In a way, Habitat became the concrete demonstration of this vision of the future. The *Expo 67 Official Guide* presents the project as follows: "Habitat 67 reveals to the fullest the extent to which man has used his ingenuity in combining shelter with all the attributes of modern life, in an urban world in which living space is at a premium."[11]

Habitat's road to becoming a theme pavilion was a bumpy one. In May 1965, the Architectural Design Branch of the Department of Installations of the Canadian Corporation for the 1967 World Exhibition (CCWE) established a committee "to determine the best possible use of 'Habitat' during Expo 67."[12] The Habitat Exhibition Use Committee, which Moshe Safdie sat on, discussed not only the allocation of commercial and residential spaces, but also the areas reserved

FIGURE 5.1

View of a Habitat '67 kitchen

for exhibitions and visitor traffic. After about a dozen meetings, the committee proposed that "36 units ... be displayed to the Exhibition visitor in the south cluster of the project."[13] In April 1966, an advisory committee[14] recommended that the Canadian Council of Furniture Manufacturers invite its members, through their provincial associations, to submit proposals for these units by 29 July, while the Toronto magazine *Chatelaine* coordinated the interior decoration.[15] At the same time, as the chief architect of the CCWE, Édouard Fiset, recalls, all aspects of the Habitat design were subject to approval by Moshe Safdie's firm in accordance with the terms of his contract. Fiset himself recommended that a consultant be hired from a qualified firm of designers to act as coordinator,[16] and Jacques Guillon was engaged for that purpose. Guillon had already worked for the CCWE and was, with Norman Hay, one of the leading members of the design team for Expo 67.[17] On their own authority, Safdie and Guillon approached several commercial attachés in the international delegations and secured the potential participation of Denmark, England, and Japan.[18] But the Canadian Council of Furniture Manufacturers put pressure on the authorities to impose strictly Canadian content and exclude any international contributions; otherwise it would withdraw from the project. The CCWE finally agreed to the idea of a completely Canadian concept.[19] Faced with opposition from Denmark, however, Expo's commissioner general, Pierre Dupuy, had to defend this position in Moscow before the International Exhibitions Bureau.[20]

The technical instructions given to representatives of *Chatelaine* specified that the interior design should be in keeping with the concept of the project but that the designers should not take too futuristic an approach in an attempt to reflect the avant-garde nature of the architecture. Instead, the concept of "good design" should dictate all aspects of the work.[21] *Chatelaine*'s proposals were rejected three times (23 August, 14 September, and 28 October 1966), after its submissions were severely criticized by Anthony A. Peters of the CCWE, Moshe Safdie, and Jacques Guillon in turn.[22] At the time of the last submission, Guillon observed sarcastically that *Chatelaine*'s proposal had a "House and Gardens type of sleek rendering. The same drab appearance in colour selection appears and the furniture is typical of the Canadian Furniture Mart's unimaginative standards."[23] Guillon then suggested that industrial designers, some of whom had already been approached, be asked to lay out one to three units in the spirit of a "total design" in keeping with the philosophy of Expo 67 and the National Design Council. This solution, then identified as Concept B, was adopted in part for thirteen of the twenty-six units, the compromise being, however, that only Canadian products would be used.[24] Meanwhile, another suite was reserved as the official residence of the commissioner general of Expo 67. Safdie was given a mandate to modify his plans accordingly and to propose an interior design in collaboration with Jacques Guillon's firm.[25]

Twelve Showcases for Canadian Design ... or Almost

The first two suites of Habitat '67 for which *Chatelaine* was responsible were unveiled to the media in February 1967. The journalists noted in particular the kitchens and bathrooms, and some expressed reservations about the not so avant-garde furniture. The journalist from *La Presse* called it "an expensive case for costume jewellery."[26] As planned, *Chatelaine* coordinated the decoration of thirteen apartments. Barbara MacLennan, a consultant to the interior decoration department of the magazine, admitted candidly that "the designs submitted by the industry were largely 'traditional,' since that group of styles accounts for about 75 percent of household furniture sales in Canada. Although this choice may seem unfortunate from the point of view of architecture or design, it had the advantage of allowing visitors to relate their own lifestyle to the revolutionary concept of the urban shown in Habitat 67."[27]

It was also in February 1967 that the designers chosen to decorate Habitat's Concept B suites had a meeting with the architect.[28] After considerable discussion, twelve units instead of thirteen were set aside for their designs. Here, the principle of Canadian exclusivity does not seem to have been fully respected, since one suite was reserved for Francisco Imported Furniture, which specialized in imports from Brazil, and another for the firm Herman Miller, where the furniture designs of Charles Eames were dominant. The second principle, to adhere to modern design or, at the very least, to one in accord with the precepts of "good design," was also partly forgotten, as some apartments were entrusted to Les Artisans du Meuble Québécois. Their diamond points and curved woodwork provided a striking contrast to the concrete cubes of Habitat '67.[29]

Among the more successful suites, one by the firm of Jacques Guillon deserves special mention. Guillon was a key player in overseeing the interior design of the building. Within his firm, the project was entrusted to the young Michel Dallaire, who had earlier worked for Julien Hébert and had recently returned from studying overseas at the Konstfackskolan, the University College of Art, Craft, and Design in Stockholm. Dallaire's colleague Jacques Coutu collaborated on the furniture for the children's room.[30] Guillon's firm first studied the spaces in order to plan the layout and dimensions of the furniture for the different rooms.[31] For the dining room, the red-lacquered, moulded plywood tripod chairs with black leather seats provided a space-saving solution for the limited floor area in the Habitat apartments. This furniture was also collapsible for easy transport.[32] The design for the living room furniture – a table, sofa, armchair, and ottoman – employed a square structure in solid oak reinforced by laminated joints at the corners. For the seating, plump cushions covered in fabric, leather, or suede rested on straps; the angle between the seat and the back could be slightly adjusted by changing the tension of the webbing that connected the floating crosspiece to one of the rear braces of the structure.[33] This furniture, which was distributed for about fifteen years by Paul Arno, could be seen until recently in the lobbies of hotels such as the Méridien (today the Hyatt Regency Montreal).

The development of a simple model for the study of angles led Guillon's firm to design, in addition to the seating described above, a garden chair for Habitat's terrace.[34] The structure of this chair is made up of two identical elements in aluminum tubing that form a rectangle with rounded corners. Jacques Guillon patented the design in September 1968. In 1974, the chair was marketed on a larger scale by the firm Karema Furniture (Figure 5.2). Offered in aluminum tubing plated in chrome or coated with epoxy in different colours, with two cushions covered in canvas or leather in a variety of colours, the "Jacques Guillon Designer's Chair," as it was then called, was delivered in a cardboard box.[35] It was among the six products chosen for an article on Canadian design published in the prestigious Italian magazine *Domus*.[36]

The Habitat '67 terraces also used a design developed by Jerry Adamson for the firm Dudas Kuypers Rowan Ltd – a rotary-moulded polyethylene armchair (Figure 5.3). The translucent material permitted an original outdoor application, for "the designers [had] discovered that a light source under the chair and the ottoman generated a soft, suffused glow throughout the entire shell. Decorative and effective low-level lighting was thus achieved on the apartment terraces by careful placement of 'glowing' chairs and ottomans."[37] For indoors, both pieces of furniture were given cushions coordinated with the other furniture. Adamson was also in charge of the design of the light fixtures, as well as the

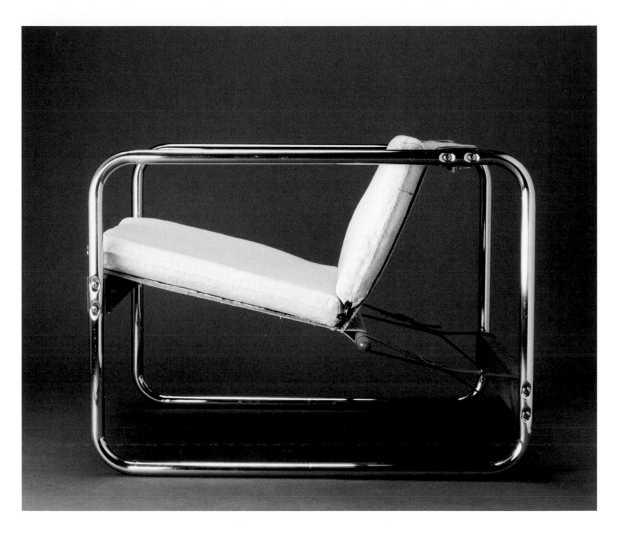

FIGURE 5.2

Jacques S. Guillon & Associates Ltd, Habitat garden chair, 1967–74
(chrome steel tube, cedar, fabric, upholstery)

FIGURE 5.3

Jerry Adamson (Dudas Kuypers Rowan Ltd) for Interiors International Ltd,
Habitat chair and ottoman, 1967 (polyethylene, upholstery)

COLLECTION OF DESIGN EXCHANGE, GIFT OF 20TH CENTURY GALLERY, 998.13
PHOTO: HARRY FOSTER, CANADIAN MUSEUM OF CIVILIZATION

furniture for the bedroom and dining room, where the chairs were similar in shape to the armchairs but were supported on aluminum tubing underframes. For these elements, he used other industrial materials, including fibreglass-reinforced plastic.[38]

The designer Jerry Adamson had been involved in the Habitat project for a long time. Moshe Safdie had approached him during the preliminary stages, when the architect hoped to design all the units.[39] For the two apartments that had been entrusted to Dudas Kuypers Rowan, Adamson conceived furniture that would be in accord with the precepts of Habitat '67 and correspond to the new lifestyles of a changing society. First of all, he rejected traditional methods of furniture making and took his inspiration from the production and assembly techniques used for the construction of Habitat.[40] Second, he designed light, stackable, modular elements that could be personalized and leased with the apartments. That, at least, was what he presented at the launch in April 1967.[41] To demonstrate the versatility of his creations, he presented two applications in the suites decorated by his firm. In the first one, for an active and extroverted family of four, the furniture was covered with a sturdy, easy to maintain, colourful fabric, while the tables were in fibreglass-reinforced plastic. In the second, for an intellectual couple, the coverings were leather or wool and the tables made of transparent acrylic.[42] A few thousand copies of the "Habitat" armchair and ottoman were later produced by John Geiger of Interiors International Ltd (today, Geiger of the Herman Miller Group). It was the first plastic chair produced commercially in Canada.[43]

Alison Hymas was asked to do another of the suites. She was associated at the time with the architectural firm of Webb Zerafa Menkes of Toronto and had previously worked with Jacques Guillon's firm in Montreal after graduating from the University of Manitoba in interior design. Hymas designed cubic furniture reflecting the architecture of Habitat '67, which, in her own words, "impose[d] a strong image of simplicity and repetition of basic forms [and] required architect-type furniture."[44] Made of 2.85 cm–thick oak plywood specially designed and produced by Craftwood Products for this project, the chairs were only briefly marketed by Keilsonn Ltd.[45] Of all the furniture designed for Habitat, Hymas' was probably the most in visual harmony with the geometry of the architectural concept that had inspired it (Figure 5.4).

David Bodrug, of the firm Forrest, Bodrug & Associates, was in charge of one of the units. His furniture was also of great geometric simplicity, combining

FIGURE 5.4

View of living room designed by Alison Hymas for Habitat '67

FROM CANADIAN INTERIORS, SEPTEMBER 1967
PHOTO: ROGER JOWETT, HAYWARD STUDIOS
COURTESY OF J. ALISON HYMAS, BID, RCA

teak and solid white oak. The living room and dining room furniture and the bedside lamp were built on a square framework and echoed the spirit of the architectural environment in which they were used. The bedroom chair, a hemisphere on a tripod, provided a break from what could have become an overly rigid formula.[46] Office Equipment of Canada applied the principles of prefabrication and the modular construction process of Habitat in furniture designed by Robert Kaiser of Takna. The dining room set had already been sold at Eaton's in Toronto in May 1966.[47] This furniture, in plywood lacquered in different colours, used neither screws nor glue; it could be completely taken apart and then reassembled by fitting together the different cut-out panels.[48]

Sigrun Bülow-Hübe's approach was completely distinct. For her, "when you enter any of these house units you find yourself in more or less traditional rooms ... the 'drama' from indoors is experienced through the windows ... Hence, I have not felt any need to create a 'dramatic' interior, nor a revolutionary one."[49] Bülow-Hübe, of Swedish origin, had come to Montreal in 1950. Along with Reinhold Koller, she worked mostly in the furniture firm Aka Works, from 1953 to 1968. Faithful to her origins, she designed for Habitat a variety of Scandinavian-inspired furniture: a rosewood chair and sofa with a chrome steel structure, a pivoting chair and daybed in moulded plywood, and teak dining room and bedroom sets (Figure 5.5). The oak bed in the children's room was convertible. Several wall units used a slightly bolder combination of wood and plastic laminate (Formica).[50]

Another designer of Scandinavian origin, Danish in this case, contributed to the project. Christen Sorensen, who had been trained in Copenhagen, had arrived in Canada in 1956 and worked with Jacques Guillon's firm from 1958 to 1962. For Habitat, he designed a few rooms of furniture produced by Ebena Lasalle, a firm he had managed a few years before. His upholstered suede couch, his hemispherical chairs, and especially his wall unit mounted on an aluminum rail were designed to minimize clutter and open up the view of the outdoors.[51]

Hugh Spencer, without doubt one of the most notable designers of his time – known especially for his "Project G" stereo for Clairtone – was also given a suite in Habitat to design. In his statement in the magazine *Canadian Interiors*, he did not hide his disappointment over the lack of time and money for this project. Spencer, who had founded the design firm Opus International in 1960, had just launched Form/Factor, a commercial company for the fabrication and distribution of his designs. His goal at the time was to develop a line of products that

FIGURE 5.5

View of living room designed by Sigrun Bülow-Hübe for Habitat '67

THE JOHN BLAND CANADIAN ARCHITECTURE COLLECTION,
MCGILL UNIVERSITY, MONTREAL; FONDS SIGRUN BÜLOW-HÜBE
PHOTO: MAX SAUER STUDIO REG'D
COURTESY OF DR JUDITH ADAMSON

FIGURE 5.6

Hugh Spencer, Club Chair U30 for Opus International, 1967
(steel, laminated rosewood, leather, upholstery)

would break down the boundaries between the domestic sphere and the business world, between home and office. His elegant chairs and sofas, in moulded laminated rosewood with metal underframes and leather coverings, were also used in the Place des Nations, for the heads of state lounge (Figure 5.6).[52] Created in the same spirit, Spencer's "Slinger" chair first drew attention during the Canadian Furniture Mart in Toronto a few months earlier.[53] While his furniture was already in production, Spencer seemed particularly proud of his original creation for Habitat, a stereo console in which the speakers were set inside poured-concrete chambers.

In spite of the political wrangling and the lack of time and money, the design of the suites in Habitat '67 provided an opportunity for a few Canadian designers to showcase their talent to the hundreds of thousands of people visiting Expo 67. Among all the products proposed, certain ones stood out: Jerry Adamson's plastic chair for its boldness, Jacques Guillon's living room furniture for its lines and its commercial success, and Hugh Spencer's chair for its elegance. Like the architectural project of Habitat '67 itself, the interior designs may not have met original expectations, but they nonetheless remain a landmark in the history of design in Canada.

same decade, different styles

6

Capsules: Plastic and Utopia

BRENT CORDNER

In an exultant display of technological and artistic fruition, the world's nations gathered at the Crystal Palace in London in 1851. By ship and by carriage, travellers arrived in London to witness the bounty of commerce installed in the prefabricated framework of an enormous vitrine. Countless ventures were launched promising the delivery of art and technology under the stewardship of God, an unlikely synthesis of faith and technology.[1] Pressed into the surface of a rubber tablet given to Prince Albert, the words of William Cowper epitomized the event:

> ... The band of commerce was design'd
> T' associate all the branches of mankind;
> And if a boundless plenty be the robe,
> Trade is the golden girdle of the globe.
> Wise to promote whatever end he means,
> God opens fruitful Nature's various scenes;
> Each climate needs what other climes produce,
> And offers something to the general use;
> No land but listens to the common call,
> And in return receives supplies from all.[2]

Amidst all the output of the world, a most extraordinary installation was Charles Goodyear's Vulcanite Court, named by him for the process he discovered

FIGURE 6.1

Charles Goodyear's drawing of internally lit, transparent rubber globes, 1853

FROM: THE APPLICATIONS AND USES OF VULCANIZED GUM-ELASTIC; WITH DESCRIPTIONS AND DIRECTIONS FOR MANUFACTURING PURPOSES, 1853

for stabilizing rubber. Installed under a semi-synthetic canopy suspended from the steel trusses of the Crystal Palace, his Vulcanite Court was the largest of the displays in the American partition of the exhibition.[3]

Goodyear created an illusory setting in the semblance of a domestic space to house all of his remarkable things: globes lighter than air (Figure 6.1), pneumatic floatation devices and boats, rubber fabric curtains that segmented the space, and all manner of domestic objects made from a hard and shiny substance that could pass for ebony or horn.[4]

Goodyear's recreation in rubber must have seemed an otherworldly place to the Victorians. Though modelled after traditional domesticity, the hard, moulded objects were defamiliarized by their semi-synthetic composition. Pneumatics filled with liquid and air bore more resemblance to fragile bodily organs than to the utilitarian implements common in other stalls. Every surface – floor, ceiling, wall, and curtain – was rubber coated,[5] constituting something previously unseen: a total work of art in one material. Part utopia and part promotional vehicle, the Vulcanic Court was the first all-plastic interior and a clear proposal that the world might be remade in some other way. It prefigured the total environments of the sixties and introduced a persistent formalism that emerges from the properties of resinous materials.

Though visionary, Goodyear's illusory world was temporary. His short-lived exhibition space was converted into a rubber-goods store when the Crystal Palace relocated to Sydenham.[6] It was only after World War II that Goodyear's vision for a plastic world became part of quotidian life.

Pneumatic airships, constructed of aluminum frames and synthetic skins, patrolled the coastline during World War II, forming a communications network that contributed to the early warning and defence system of the United States.

Plastics played a considerable role in the war and both sides relied on it. An increase in research caused an explosion of new materials.[7] "Plastic" became an umbrella term for a family of materials with divergent properties. The new synthetics were selected for their performance, and they replaced materials that were in short supply. The variety of applications was extensive: every handle grip, blood bag, water canteen, gas mask, dial indicator, raincoat, shatterproof cockpit, and life-preserver brought the soldier into contact with an essential application of the material. The versatility of plastic placed it in good stead.

Postwar prosperity fostered a climate of enthusiasm marked by faith in technology and a fervent belief in the free market system. A vision of a wondrous future built out of the new material was promoted by industry. Some envisioned an ideal future in which plastics would be derived entirely from plant materials and cars would be grown from the soil.[8] A "Plastics Age" was imminent, when, foreseeably, the production of plastic would surpass the extraction of iron.[9] The blimps no longer patrolled the coasts – they patrolled public gatherings and football games, sporting logos.

Many of the solutions to the challenges of equipping, feeding, and transporting soldiers in World War II were applied to everyday living in a newly affluent society.[10] Now perfected, plastic films played an unprecedented role in the delivery of perishable food thanks to their convenience, disposability, and low cost. By the late fifties and early sixties, *Modern Packaging* magazine showed that ads for plastics had gained ground on those for paper and aluminum. Common descriptors could no longer adequately describe the new profusion of chemically derived materials, necessitating the invention of trade names, a peculiar new form of nomenclature that was part science, part popular appeal. Brodart, Plyofilm, Vinylite ... by 1959 there were over ten thousand such trade names covering applications as diverse as medication, adhesives, cleansers, fertilizers, and polymers.[11]

With its myriad applications, all seemingly positive, plastic insinuated itself into the public's consciousness as a benevolent presence. Electronic entertainment had invaded the household in the form of televisions cased in bakelite and radios in colourful urea formaldehyde. The abundance of the supermarket was delivered shrink-wrapped and preserved at home in Tupperware. Hygiene came in blow-moulded containers; health, in dissolvable caplets.

Technological advances in the plastics industry coupled with the construction of a positive identity were the necessary preconditions for plastic's widespread adoption as an alternative to traditional materials. The identity of plastic had become a complex interplay of signs relating to transport, delivery, provision, protection, and convenience, all associated with the most affirmative consequence of industrial production: abundance. The focus of our most primal desires, abundance is a necessary outcome of utopian thinking.[12] Not coincidentally, the essential message of all advertising is the promise of a better future, a promotional message that was clinging to plastic as it entered the sixties.

A generation of disaffected youth raised with Lego and water wings seized the initiative to symbolically overturn previous ways of living by recreating the domestic object and its surrounding space. It took a counterculture[13] to decide that the steel, leather, and bent plywood of the modern movement should be displaced by some alternative. The demographic surge of youth took its stance by seizing the material of the future and applying it to every surface.

In 1959 *The Package*, an exhibition held at the Museum of Modern Art in New York, signalled that, for the first time, the design of packaging was a topic deserving of an assessment. Whereas packaging had previously been an exercise in graphic design, it had suddenly become a pursuit for the industrial designer. The content of the exhibition – the blow-moulded containers, the blister packs, and other forms of dispensers – revealed the full maturation of plastic film and packaging, and an industrial complex poised to inundate the market with a profusion of consumer products with unprecedented efficiency.

In the introduction of the exhibition catalogue, Arthur Drexler equated the design of the plastic radio casing with the design of packaging when he stated, "The casing for a radio ... protects delicate parts but must be designed somewhat in the manner of a printed page or box."[14] The shelling of electrical devices with plastic brought about a convergence in two previously distinct types of output – the domestic object and disposable waste. Drexler fulminated against the built-in obsolescence dictated by fashion and the design of the "object as a package in the commercial sense: a gaudy wrapping intended to catch the eye,"[15] tendencies that were later embraced by the pop design movement.

If pop art appropriated the imagery of consumer culture,[16] then pop furniture declared its affinity to packaging. The convergence of the permanent and the disposable resulted in an "aesthetic of disposability,"[17] conferring to the domestic object a state of semi-permanence. Never before had one material been applied to domestic objects with the symbolic stature of the chair while also serving predominantly as disposable packaging – a confounding paradox that afflicts the identity of plastic to this day.

The propensity for plastic to form containers emerged not only from the properties of its various incarnations, but also from its various manufacturing processes. Contrary to the modernist expression of parts, plastic could flow or bend around corners, forming cavitated volumes (Figure 6.2). Rotational moulding formed hollow objects with uninterrupted surfaces. Injection-moulding imbued the object with the qualities of a vessel. Plastic films and textiles enveloped air and foam.

Since molten plastic took the shape of its container, every moulded object was a coating that formed on the inside of a volume. The necessity of the draft angle for successful withdrawal of the male part of the mould gave the ensuing object the tendency to stack, nest, or form some modular assemblage. Repetition became legible in the surface of every plastic object.

Owing to the high cost of research, refining, synthesizing, and machining, plastic was rooted in industrial production. Manufacturing processes demanded the production of sufficient volume to offset the upfront capital cost of tooling, ensuring that plenty was available to all. The stacking plastic object embodied

FIGURE 6.2

Robert Forrest, 2001 Chair for L'image Design, 1969
(bronzed tubing, acrylic shell, feather and down-filled wool cushions)

COLLECTION OF DESIGN EXCHANGE, GIFT OF HONEY AND ALAN STARK, 2001.2
PHOTO: PETE PATERSON
COURTESY OF PETE PATERSON

the confluence of utopian abundance and the industrial pursuit of profit. From its inception, plastic has had to contend with this paradox, making anti-consumerist expressions in plastic insupportable.

The culmination of utopianism in the sixties occurred in the all-plastic interior. It posited a total other place while it simultaneously denied the existence of the real world by removing the participant to a place of fiction.

In 1965 an extraordinary place was installed in the basement of a four-storey stone edifice in Montreal by an unlikely client and an unusual designer (Figure 6.3). The owners of a chain of pharmacies called "Le Drug" approached a young François Dallegret to design and build a café-bar beneath one of their existing stores. A superstructure of tubes, shelves, and bold graphic signs were erected on the first floor to invigorate the display of the pharmacy, but the basement was transformed into something altogether different. Dallegret conceived an envelope within the existing building that concealed the solidity of the basement walls. A gleaming and convoluted gossamer absorbed patrons into the underground space. Removed from the familiar commerce of the street, they were deposited into a place that encouraged other forms of participation. Enveloped by wall-banquettes, people formed clusters around tables that merged into the floor. It was a space that defied the idea of commodity by fusing all of the components of the space into a continuous surface. Those things that were removable, the dispensers for sugar and cream, dispelled the illusion by reminding the participants of the world outside. The fiction of the all-plastic expression lay just beneath the surface, as ordinary wood and iron bistro tables, coated with lathe and concrete, were used to prop it up; an insubstantial coating of plastic resin concealed the ruse.

Dallegret's beautiful vision did not last long. It was dismantled by the owners after only two years, for the most mundane but necessary reason: it was impossibly expensive to maintain. The pristine white surface required the frequent attention of a cleaning crew because it was prone to being scuffed by black rubber-soled shoes.

Buckminster Fuller identified two paradigms of pre-modern construction: the fortress and the ship.[18] The fortress was the earth-bound bastion of agrarian society that served as a defensible place and a proprietary marker, while the ship was the vector of commerce, transporting material from places of abun-

FIGURE 6.3

© FRANÇOIS DALLEGRET/SODRAC (MONTREAL) 2004

François Dallegret, Le Drug discothèque, 1965

PHOTO: BRUNO MASSENET

FIGURE 6.4

Model of Buckminster Fuller's design for the United States of America Pavilion, Montreal World's Fair, 1967

dance to places of scarcity.[19] Lightweight and temporary, the ship was designed for performance, accruing vast amounts of wealth for the merchant.[20] During the Industrial Revolution, the factory became the modern equivalent to the ship,[21] and like the ship, it only needed to last long enough to generate sufficient profit before it expired.

Fuller's American pavilion at Expo 67 was such a vessel (Figure 6.4). Assembled from prefabricated aluminum latticework infilled with hexagonal acrylic panels, Fuller's globe commanded the attention of the assembled throng with its geometric purity, a showcase of American culture and technological capability. Situated adjacent to the permanent construction of the Soviet fortress, the American ship declared the space race already won. Inside was a display of the most important facets of American export at the apex of the Cold War along with a secret weapon with which the Soviets could never contend – Hollywood glamour. It was a curious juxtaposition of popular culture and the Cold War, the two-dimensional world of celluloid represented in poster format next to the technological splendour of the space race. After having lost the first leg of the space race, the Americans outmanoeuvred the Soviets by trumping Yuri Gagarin with Marlon Brando – the former an ambassador and the latter a sales representative. The collision of the two worlds was set against the backdrop of the larger exposition, titled *Man and His World*. Its theme, prophetically, was man's stewardship of the earth.

The bubble burst in 1973 when the OPEC embargo caused a surge in the price of plastic, revealing the industry's reliance on petrochemicals.[22] The utopia of a farm-grown plastic world had never materialized. The high price of oil decimated the industry, causing a drought that lasted until the 1990s. Abundance was viewed as excess. Plastic, the miracle material of the previous decade, was suddenly viewed with distrust. The interest was no longer in the material and its formal possibilities, but in the ethics of conservation and ergonomics.[23] The exuberance that had marked the previous decade came to an end.

François Dallegret captured the idealism of the decade in his drawing of an "Environment-Bubble," in which both he and Reyner Banham appear as willing subjects (Figure 6.5). The bubble serves as an emblem for the utopian aspirations of pneumatics, as well as other all-plastic spaces in the sixties, by illustrating the fiction of such expressions.

Utopia is always a destination that entails travel.[24] Like Thomas More's distant island, Dallegret's bubble is removed from the world on a mountaintop perch, where it rests in gentle conformity with its surroundings. The distance between utopia and the world is necessary to preserve the illusion of independence. A physical barrier further confines the place so that the experiment does not escape the crucible. Inside, a set of principles governing the participants gives rise to normative behaviours – in this case nudism.

Utopia is selective and prescriptive, and the all-plastic expression is its corollary. Much as the unruly inhabitant is encouraged to leave the island, non-plastic objects don't fit in the total plastic environment. This suited the aims of a movement that had decided to purge all signs of modern rationalism.

FIGURE 6.5

François Dallegret, *The Environment-Bubble*, 1965

No material endures such highs and lows as plastic. Attitudes toward the material shift radically and quickly because, comparatively, it is still in its infancy. Wood, stone, glass, metal, and fibres are ancient to us, their identities secured by thousands of years of knowing application. The identity of plastic has not yet achieved equilibrium.

The inception of plastic coincided with the ascendance of commercialism in the mid-nineteenth century, and the material experienced its zenith in the sixties under comparable circumstances. A confluence of social and technological developments made plastic the nominal material of the decade. Plastic acquired its fortified identity following successful trials during World War II and its subsequent association with abundance. Commerce, plenty, trade, use – those same words that were imprinted in a rubber tablet in 1851 were just as integral to the identity of plastic as it entered the sixties.

Plastic was the counterpart of utopia. It complemented the expression of an ideal future because the vessel-like forms that emerged from its properties found agreement in how an abstract concept such as utopia was formalized. The hermetic capacity of plastic married well with the insular requirements of sixties utopianism – material, form, and idea coalesced into ideal representations.

Utopia is the expression of an alternative, and plastic was the alternative material. Its availability was necessary for change to have happened at all. Its versatility fuelled the creation of an immeasurable variety of forms, without which pluralism might not have been a discernible outcome of the decade.

The interplay between utopia and commerciality is the one constancy that connects the various expressions, including those of Dallegret and Fuller. Each form expressed a different utopian vision through the medium of the material. For Fuller, it was technological ascendance; for Dallegret, it was a womb-like retreat. Each ideal was realized via a material rooted in industrial production and dependent on structures that were both physical and social.

The identity of plastic was constructed by the sum total of its applications over time and by the manner in which it was represented in other texts. The material carried with it a set of signs that infused the meaning of the forms that were generated. This process was essential to the formation of the pop sensibility in design, but it contributed to plastic's subsequent downfall, with all its contradictory messages.

7

Deign to Be Modern:
Canada's Taste for Scandinavian
Design in the Sixties

MICHAEL PROKOPOW

In the fall of 1958, the Junior Auxiliary of the Toronto Symphony Orchestra Association held an exhibition called *The Decorators' Show* at the Royal Ontario Museum (ROM). Organized to raise money for the orchestra, the event was, as the small program explained to its readers, "a chance of presenting to you the work of many of Ontario's leading Interior Designers." Composed of sixteen vignettes, or small displays of furnishings and accessories, and eight large themed "rooms," the exhibition was a clear indication of the prevailing, overwhelmingly conservative tastes of the Toronto establishment.[1] Of the twenty-four display spaces at the exhibit, only one presented what visitors would have recognized as modern furnishings. The majority of the displays were period pieces – scripted studies in decorum and cautious good taste – with one or two display rooms seeking to combine the old with the new. However, as the Toronto designer Margit Bennett knew as she put together her display at *The Decorators Show* – cozy as it was with its "comfortable Danish chair," its "Swedish teak string bookshelves" and matching desk, modernism's popularity in Canada turned on much more than simply a consumer's embrace of the latest trend in home furnishings. Rather, just as modernism was positively associated – both ideologically and aesthetically – with ideas about postwar reconstruction in North America, so new forms in architecture, furnishings, accessories, and fashions were seen by those so inclined as the messengers of enlightenment (Figure 7.1).[2]

Canadian consumers in the decades after World War II faced two basic, but diametrically opposed, choices around the decoration of their homes.

FIGURE 7.1

Installation of *The Decorators' Show* at the Royal Ontario Museum, 1958

IMAGE PROVIDED BY THE ROYAL ONTARIO MUSEUM, FROM THE DECORATORS' SHOW, 1958
COURTESY OF THE ASSOCIATION OF REGISTERED INTERIOR DESIGNERS OF ONTARIO

Householders could maintain their preferences for furniture that looked old and that carried the associations of history or they could embrace modernism in all its newness. Indeed, the choices were stark. Consumers could remain tied to the past by preferring traditional styles – those colonial and provincial sofa sets with their carved wood frames and brocade upholstery and those formal dining room sets with their manufactured patinas and their Florentine, Jacobean, or Louis Quatorze allusions – or they could choose furniture that celebrated new forms and ways of living by emphasizing clean lines and eschewing decoration in any form. Modernism's transformation of Canadian domestic space – and the embrace of what was broadly labelled as Scandinavian design in particular – represented a critically important moment in the nation's postwar ideological, social, and cultural history. Thus, Scandinavian design's ascendance as the style of forward-looking, forward-thinking people represented nothing short of aesthetic revolution. And arguably, the well-heeled people of good taste who perused Bennett's singular room at the ROM had an inkling of this, even if some of them were discomforted by the thought.

Accordingly, Canada's rapid embrace of Scandinavian design as the style of choice in the late 1950s and into the new decade was but part of the country's determination to be a modern nation. The dramatically increased presence in home decoration and architectural magazines, in stores and in houses, of teak settees, pendant glass light fixtures, Flokati rugs, and Marimekko table linens among thousands of other consumer products was the domestic manifestation of the modernizing mission that produced skyscrapers, freeways, sleek airports, and reassuring, if endless, CMHC (Central Mortgage and Housing Corporation) suburbs. As a result, the sixties were the decade where many Canadians sought to align their private material lives with what they regarded as the greater forces of positive social change.[3]

That Scandinavian modernism – both in its authentic forms and in the loose domestic interpretations of it that followed – became the signature style of the sixties raises questions about what it was about this aesthetic that appealed so powerfully to so many Canadians. Part of the answer lies in the fact that the nation's sensibility – restrained, communitarian, and northern – found resonance in Scandinavian aesthetics. The celebration of the simple that was a hallmark of Nordic aesthetic culture, not to mention the brilliant translation of the craft sensibility in the mass production of beautiful everyday objects, appealed logically to many Canadians. With their generally modest means and predisposition against ostentation, Canadians found the inherent rationality and egalitarian qualities of Scandinavian design fitting for a country that prided itself on its European heritage and temperament and that was always conflicted with following the American model of postwar modernity.[4]

To this end, style-conscious and nationalistic Canadian consumers of a particular type drove the popularity of Scandinavian design, or what came to be generically known as "Danish modern." Seeking to combine economy with style and to remain true to their senses of self, homemakers – many of them born before the war and coming of age in the late fifties and early sixties – sought to make their small living rooms spacious, their bedrooms light and airy, their dining rooms elegant but friendly, and their children's rooms formative but playful. The versatility and appeal of modern design meant that the marketplace went to great lengths to accommodate the public's material needs. Importers and manufacturers alike kept apace of consumer desires by selling and making things of all descriptions – from daybeds to fondue pots – and modern-minded shoppers across the country and the income spectrum found themselves able to decorate their homes according to the latest Nordic and Nordic-inspired taste.

And, any homemaker's quick browse of *Canadian Homes and Gardens*, *Western Homes and Living*, or *Canadian Interiors* would have revealed the extent to which Scandinavian modern had infiltrated the nation's decorating psyche after 1960. Advertisements for modernism of all sorts jostled with ads for French provincial, Spanish colonial, and Georgian traditional pieces.[5] And while an advertisement for "Richelieu" dining-room furniture made by the Elmira-Snyder furniture company of Waterloo, Ontario, could speak of "elegant modern day living, with an old world touch and twentieth century requirements," the fact that the ad was situated close to advertisements showing the modernity of modernism only accentuated the seeming anachronistic quality of the historically styled table, chairs, and hutch.[6] For most consumers, however, the various advertisements tended to confirm already-held tastes rather than convert them to new and different ones. As such, the advertisements for modern furniture and objects, whether made in Finland or Sweden, or styled as Swedish by such Canadian designers and firms as Sigrun Bülow-Hübe, Walter Nugent, Kaufman, and Imperial, while revealing the range of quality in the products presented and parading as contemporary, nonetheless spoke to the coherence of the modernist aesthetic (Figure 7.2).[7] The triumph of Danish modern in Canada was the

FIGURE 7.2

Staff designers, armchair for Imperial Contemporary, c. 1962 (teak, upholstery)

ease with which homemakers – whether married couples or singles – could fashion stylish, contemporary interiors that were comfortable, inviting and distinct. But always more than simply a matter of personal taste, the decision to go modern – while a powerful impulse in Canadian society in the early sixties – did imply a progressive and advanced thinking about the meaning of objects in everyday life and how issues of style were in truth issues of identity.

And interested consumers did have a vast range of products from which to choose. In the retail section of the January 1962 edition of *Canadian Homes and Gardens*, for example, consumers were given the opportunity to ponder the merits of a stylish cheeseboard from Georg Jensen Ltd, painted ceramics from Norway, and a prone figurine by Danish ceramicist Lisa Larsen capable of being used either as a paperweight or a bookend.[8] Similarly, the July issue boasted an advertisement for Gense's "Focus De Luxe" flatware. Designed by Folke Arnstrom, the Gense cutlery was celebrated for its sleek styling – stainless tines, blades, and bowls with black resin handles – and for the fact that its radical form heralded the demise of old-fashioned tableware. That it was identified as the "world's costliest stainless" did not seem to matter, the implication being that no price was too high for high style.[9]

Indeed, while promoting good taste and design in the household across the board, *Canadian Homes and Gardens* had a clear predilection for Scandinavian modernism. Moreover, staff designer Margit Bennett was an extremely powerful national taste-maker. From 1958 through to 1962, for example, she offered readers of *Canadian Homes and Gardens* a review of the latest offerings of furniture manufacturers and retailers. With their elaborately staged photo shoots, perhaps on some loading dock, Bennett and several colleagues from the design establishment would vet the eclectic range of products available to consumers. However, readers of Bennett's commentaries on design would have recognized the modern inclinations of her taste.

Bennett's columns on décor, available products, and how to use good design in the decorating of one's home were staples of the magazine's campaign to promote the make-over of domestic interiors in a modern vein (Figure 7.3). For example, an article appearing in the June 1962 issue offered readers advice on "How to Make Your Summer Cottage Sunny Inside," confirming the appropriateness and appeal of modern design in everyday settings.[10] Written with the help of decorator Peter Keay, Bennett's piece extolled the virtues of keeping decorating simple and asserted that there existed a stylistic coherence among

the items assembled. In addition, the writers offered that castoffs should be avoided, that the budget was always of prime importance, that "an occasional touch of luxury be added," and that accessories be "lively." Bennett and Keay recommended any number of lively Scandinavian products for the location-less cottage. Included were the black-striped, brown-edged Spisa cups and saucers by Stig Lindberg for Gustavsberg, simple pine plank benches for the living room, various Norwegian and Swedish pottery kitchen pieces, and elegant black wrought-iron and enamel candle holders. The effect – as clearly intended by the designers – was one of affable and affordable leisure, mindful that cottages were significant allocations of household resources.[11]

Arguably, issues of comfort and attainability lay at the heart of the lure of Scandinavian design for Canadians in the sixties. With the plethora of Canadian-made objects that embraced the aesthetic and philosophical principles of Scandinavian design culture – monochromatic colours, restrained bio-morphism, and the attendant freedom to create spaces in ways that reflected personal taste as opposed to the following of convention – it was a case of the times suiting the style and the style suiting the times. As such, most home decorating magazines promoted Scandinavian design as the natural choice of sensible modern people.

Indeed, a lead story in the same issue that featured Bennett's lakeside retreat showed the stylish reliability of Danish modern and Danish-styled furnishings in a family setting. Concerned mainly with issues of space, flow, and the realities of adults and children living together, the article about Frank and Jean

FIGURE 7.4

View of the Harringtons' dining room and living room

FROM CANADIAN HOMES AND GARDENS, JUNE 1962
PHOTO: CLIVE WEBSTER AND JOHN HOLMES
COURTESY OF CLIVE WEBSTER

Harrington's modern bungalow in Halifax nevertheless was a showcase for the casual comfort afforded by modern furnishings. The article's successful discussion of the relatively open-plan living room and dining room turned on the 180-degree photograph "taken from master-bedroom doorway" that captured the bright and commodious public spaces (Figure 7.4). From left to right, the viewer sees the family dining room – set for an intimate dinner for two, with woven placemats and stylized floral china – and then the living room, where housewife Jean and architect Frank sit reading. As for the Harringtons' possessions profiled in the photograph, the majority of the pieces were modern, and while not all were by name designers, they nonetheless embodied the principles of easy-to-manage comfort and style that were the hallmarks of the Scandinavian moment in Canadian domestic history. The dining room, for example, had a low credenza, an elliptical teak table, four matching chairs with curved backrests, and a long, low bookcase that at the same time served as the barrier to the cathedral stairwell. In the living room, an upholstered sofa sat against and was anchored by a simple coffee table with canted legs. Immediately to the right of the sofa, situated in front of the sliding glass doors that opened on to the sundeck, were two Finn Juhl–like lounge chairs, examples of the ubiquitous, low-slung teak, walnut, or rosewood chairs with detached pillows for the seat and back. To the left of the free-standing metal fireplace was an upholstered reading chair with a tall back reminiscent of the work of Hans Wegner and others. Taken together and given their being situated in a flat-roofed, heavily fenestrated house, the furnishings of the two rooms confirmed that the Harringtons – solid family people – could celebrate the responsibilities and traditions of family while living a modern life. As for the moulded fibreglass chairs by Charles Eames, the lamp with the painted floral base, and the potted philodendron, it is likely that most readers were comforted by the current familiarity of it all and the fact that the aesthetic rules of Canadian modernism were sufficiently flexible for traditional pieces – as well as icons of American mid-century design – to be included in the decoration of the room.[12]

To be sure, the themes of family and the accommodating capacities of modernism were to be found consistently in publications from coast to coast. For example, readers of *Western Homes and Living* (a much-respected décor magazine that saw its market as stretching from Winnipeg west to the Pacific) were not only shown the latest architectural trends – with the modernist houses of Arthur Erickson and others figuring prominently – but were likewise offered information on the latest and best products for the decoration of their homes. The "Shoppers' Bazarre" section of the magazine offered viewers useful information about design and the availability of modern furnishings and accents in several urban centres. In October 1966, for example, writer Brigid Anne Clarke discussed the merits of a "luxurious swivel chair" and ottoman from Denmark upholstered in black leather (Figure 7.5). Aimed towards the man of the family, Clarke's text noted that the chair offered an escape from the "pressures and strains of a hectic business." Clarke went so far as to suggest that "testing" the chair – available at New Look Interiors, Vancouver's premier purveyor of Danish design – was "a tonic in itself." Perhaps not surprisingly, directly adjacent to the clearly gendered advertisement for a man's chair was an advertisement for dishware and the like aimed squarely at the lady of the house. Placed by Jorgen's Danish Interiors of Vancouver, the advertisement relied on a cramped little photograph of the store's interior. Accompanied by text noting that "no photograph could do justice to the exquisite display of imported Danish china, glasswear [*sic*], table lamps, etc.," the image revealed a shop floor with row upon row

FIGURE 7.5

"Luxurious swivel chair" and ottoman from Denmark, upholstered in black leather

FROM WESTERN HOMES AND LIVING, OCTOBER 1966

of open shelving stacked with all manner of Scandinavian housewares. To the knowing eye, Krenit enameled bowls could be seen jostling for space next to Sarpeneva cast-iron pots and Arabia cow creamers. As the ad suggested, for the hostess interested in having a "well-appointed home" suited to "gracious living and entertaining," Jorgen's was the right destination.[13] Similarly catchy illustrated advertisements and clever pitches for modern furniture filled the pages of the monthly, with consumers everywhere being educated in the ways of modern existence.

Thus, from about 1960 onward, the Canadian homemaker – whether in Ottawa, Victoria, or Moncton – could not have helped but be aware of the aesthetic trend towards Scandinavian modern that had taken such firm hold in the

FIGURE 7.6

Lotte Bostlund, *Table Lamp #1803* for Bostlund Industries, 1964 (cast-moulded stone-ware, filament-wound fibreglass)

COLLECTION OF THE CANADIAN MUSEUM OF CIVILIZATION, 2004.6.1

PHOTO: HARRY FOSTER, CANADIAN MUSEUM OF CIVILIZATION

COURTESY OF THE ESTATE OF LOTTE BOSTLUND (MORTEN BOSTLUND)

nation. It was, to be sure, the most powerful aesthetic force in Canadian domestic culture in the decade marked by Pearson's diplomacy, Trudeau's humane social vision, and the centennial birthday party in Montreal that alerted the world to the fact that Canada, usually so quiet and unassuming, was hip, thoughtful, passionate, and stylish. The broad popularity of what was regarded as Scandinavian modern was one of several indications of a conservative nation's willingness to be modern in a time of great change, but modern on its own culturally specific terms (Figure 7.6). And arguably, Margit Bennett sensed this when she constructed her gentle display of modern living at the ROM amidst the chintz and the Chippendale. The success of a democratic nation rested on the diversity of opinion and the freedom of choice. For Bennett, as for other aesthetically minded persons, modern design was but one option among many and one could make of it what one wished.[14] And although Bennett's modern foray at the decorating show was stylistically isolated, the message was clear. One could persist in a fondness for Queen Anne, Tudor, or Rococo-revival and presume that the past had a legitimate place in contemporary life or one could embrace a new material order of things that looked to a future freed of pretension and the belief in outdated ways of doing things and of living.

Of course, like all stylistic movements, the enthusiasm for all things Scandinavian in the sixties was destined to become simply a passing phase in the history of taste and aesthetic change. That Scandinavian furnishings and objects continued to be advertised and celebrated in the popular press well into the next decade was to be expected, as was the fact that the pure lines of Danish and Swedish originals became diluted and weak simulacra. Moreover, that companies like Gibbard and Elmira-Snyder, among so many others, could successfully continue to manufacture furniture that harkened back to a romanticized past was simply part of contemporary society's ever-ongoing negotiation with history. If anything, Canadian consumers – the masses of solid citizens interested in making homes for their families and themselves – sought out furnishings that fit their personalities and identities, whether inherited or newly fashioned. Scandinavian and Scandinavian-inspired design was, in truth, simply a moment in aesthetic time that captured the prevailing mood of the nation. Never doctrinaire, rarely exclusionary, and ultimately gentle in its presence, the style in its broad manifestations became the appropriate material embodiment of a dynamic nation at a particularly dynamic moment in history.

8

When Counterculture
Went Mainstream

ALAN C. ELDER

In every generation, Canadians have had to rework the miracle of their political existence.
Canada has been created because there has existed within the hearts of its people
a determination to build themselves an enduring home.[1]

The image is a familiar one: the location appears rural, if not wild; the hair, long and slightly dishevelled; the footwear is open-toed – probably handmade; a can of tobacco sits on a rock – rolling papers can't be far away. At the front of the image, a piece of macramé supported from a tree branch hangs over the opening in the rocks, announcing the location of a rudimentary shelter (Figure 8.1).

The image captured in the photograph appears to be stereotypical of Canada's counterculture from the sixties. It is a photograph of the generation's youths, those that Arthur Lower claimed would "rework" the nation. From the image, one would assume that Canada's young people had rejected the modern urban life of their postwar parents and taken up the romantic notion of communal rural existence that is central to legend of the sixties – a decade of upheaval and change. But the photograph also problematizes the place of craft activity in the sixties. Although seen as being part of the nation's thriving counterculture, craft was quickly being incorporated into the mainstream. In 1965 Jon Ruddy wrote about this group of young Canadians, saying:

They are concerned with marijuana, other kicks, the Bomb, each other, chess, Zen Buddhism, We Shall Overcome, pacifism, Bob Dylan psychiatry, LSD and psychedelic

FIGURE 8.1

First-year students from the University of British Columbia's School of Architecture

COLLECTION OF THE UNIVERSITY OF BRITISH COLUMBIA SCHOOL OF ARCHITECTURE
PHOTO: HENNING WULFF

experience, sex, poetry, pickets, police, sit-ins, minorities, crafts, travel, art, brotherhood and guitars.[2]

Many Canadians joined with like-minded individuals from other nations – specifically the United States – to "return to the land."[3] From coast to coast, they purchased rural properties together; they planned on living communally, eschewing the model of the nuclear family in favour of a larger tribal community structure. According to Myrna Kostash in her book *Long Way from Home*, the population of British Columbia's rural Slocan Valley increased from 420 in 1966 to 2,861 in 1971 (before that it had been decreasing since 1956).[4] The inhabitants of these "communes" rejected the consumerism of the middle class, and vowed to use only those items that were necessary for daily living. They baked bread, sowed fields, made soap (and love), played music, were wary of advancing technology, and turned to creative efforts to furnish their living environments, some of which involved trading for money or goods. Craft-based production contributed immensely to these efforts. Techniques unearthed from Western and non-Western traditions were excavated for use by contemporary makers. But not only were techniques reused, materials too were often re-appropriated by a culture that was concerned about the environmental impact of contemporaneous consumer society. Houses were constructed using "junk-yard" materials, and articles about updating old furniture appeared in homes magazines.[5]

But the image reproduced with this article does not show two people who have rejected modern urban life and returned to the Canadian landscape. The photograph shows two new students from the University of British Columbia's School of Architecture. As part of their initial project – likely intended to build alliances as well as structures – students were given basic supplies and told to create an environment they could live in. These were young people who, by their choice of architecture as a field of study, had acknowledged the existence of an urban environment. And while they may have rejected modernism's approach to urban design, they would be working in its shadow, always confronting modern innovations in materials and engineering.

Their incorporation of macramé – usually thought to be the medium of choice for hippie couples living in Volkswagen buses on rural acreage – as well as elements of their attire, indicates the importance of the handmade in the later years of the sixties. The counterculture, and the craft media that accompanied it, had become part of Canada's cultural mainstream. Rather than being relegated to the rural margins, craft was part of the vital urban scene. According to Kostash,

Notwithstanding the groups down on the farm, the counterculture was an urban affair. It was in the cities that hippies congregated to live in communal houses, work at odd jobs, deal dope, hustle gigs and just hang out; they would hit the highway to get to another city and there join precisely the same hippie society they had left behind.[6]

From Vancouver's 4th Avenue to Toronto's Yorkville to Montreal's Crescent and Mountain Streets – and places in between – "villages" of counterculture youth were formed in Canada's cities. Along with inexpensive accommodation – where Ian and Sylvia's "Four Strong Winds" could be heard mixed with Buffalo Springfield's "I think it's time we stop, children, what's that sound? / Everybody look what's going down"[7] – a network of shops and cafes were established to reinforce communal social activities. These boutiques and coffee shops catered not only to hippie youth, but also to others who were concerned with environmental issues, politics, a wide range of religions, and contemporary cultural practices. As well, group actions – sit-ins, love-ins, be-ins – drew the attention of the mainstream. Large numbers of the public attended more conservative activities, such as the Mariposa Folk Festival on the Toronto Islands and Vancouver's Studio Fairs. At these events, live entertainment, foods from other continents, and crafts went hand in hand, providing an environment that catered to counterculture and mainstream simultaneously.

This surge in attention to the handmade was also a boon to established craftspeople and craft organizations. Activities that had previously been considered as marginal now came to the forefront. Toronto's Royal Ontario Museum worked together with the Canadian Guild of Crafts (Ontario) to produce *Craft Dimensions Canada* in 1969. The exhibition, which was supported by the Canada Council for the Arts, was juried by three craftspeople from the United States. One of the jurors, textile artist Glen Kaufman, stated that the entries provided "an impression of awakening excitement in Canadian crafts"[8] at the dawn of the "Age of Aquarius."

Included in the exhibition was a table and lamp in PVC and sheet plastic by Donald Lloyd McKinley (Figure 8.2). McKinley was not a draft-dodger or wandering youth when he came to Canada in 1967, though he shared many of the concerns of members of Canada's counterculture. He was part of the generation

FIGURE 8.2

Donald Lloyd McKinley, swivel-arm double lamp and stand, 1969 (white PVC tubing)

PHOTO: D.L. MCKINLEY
COURTESY OF LYN WIGGINS

over thirty, a group that supposedly was not to be trusted by a younger generation. He came to Mississauga, Ontario, to head up the Ontario Craft Foundation's School of Design in Lorne Park.[9] This school, which later became Sheridan College's School of Crafts and Design, provided Ontario's broadest range of craft education.

McKinley had had training in both production and one-of-a-kind furniture design. He had worked as a designer at the Gunlocke Chair Company in Wayland, New York, and had received a Fulbright Scholarship in Furniture and Interior Design to study at the Ateneum in Helsinki, Finland. These two different approaches to furniture design and making were brought together in much of his work.

McKinley had started using found materials in his work while he was still in the United States. His "PVC Chaise and Ottoman" were purchased for the S.C. Johnson collection and travelled as part of *Objects USA*, an exhibition of the United States Information Service.[10] McKinley continued his exploration of PVC as a material for furniture construction when he arrived in Canada. He fused lengths of pipe together and then cut them to provide either an undulating surface for a chair or a flat surface for a table.

McKinley's reuse of materials can also be seen in his use of tin cans for tables and cardboard for chairs. In 1969 *Canadian Homes* magazine featured a McKinley chair that had as its base a cardboard tube normally used for casting concrete – a Sonotube. The tube was cut at an angle, and a brightly coloured canvas sling was slid over top. Through designs that reused "disposable" products, McKinley echoed the environmental concerns of Canadian counterculture within a post-war consumer society.

Also included in *Craft Dimensions Canada* was a stoneware planter by Harlan House (Figure 8.3). At the time, House was a student at the Alberta College of Art. Throughout the sixties and seventies, he concentrated on the production of large murals and architectural commissions. While his planter is an autonomous object, it was made on an architectural scale – suitable for large spaces. The presence of large-scale crafts in government buildings and in the offices of large corporations reflected the growing institutionalization of countercultural practices. But the work did not reflect a slick corporate profile; instead it reflected a quirky individualism that was gaining acceptance, thanks – in no small part – to the increased acceptance of other voices in society. The sixties saw increased attention given to Canadians' individual identity and rights. The

FIGURE 8.3

Harlan House, planter, 1969 (stoneware)

COLLECTION OF ONTARIO CRAFTS COUNCIL
PHOTO: HARRY FOSTER, CANADIAN MUSEUM OF CIVILIZATION
COURTESY OF HARLAN HOUSE

Quebec separatist movement, women's liberation, and gay and Native rights were much discussed in Crescent Street's cafés and in Parliament. Suddenly, personal identity issues seemed to overtake the struggle for national identity in Canada. The editors of *Maclean's* magazine addressed the rise of identity politics in an editorial in its January 1969 issue when they identified "the birth of a totally new historical phenomenon: the emergence of the individual, and his [*sic*] right to self-development, as the determining factor in history."[11]

The cultural practices of the country reflected the importance of the individual in society. Much of the ceramic work from the sixties does not reflect the precision of the previously popular work inspired by Bernard Leach. Leach, who had studied and written about Asian ceramic traditions, had influenced a large number of Canadian ceramists, particularly on the West Coast. Much of the work from Leach's St Ives–based studio was production ware that favoured repetition in form and decoration. Many ceramists in the sixties preferred a more expressive approach to their medium.

Alberta's Ed Drahanchuk, on the other hand, was able to turn his studio production into a business that aligned itself with design. A series of his works, including a lamp base and planter, were featured as part of the National Design Council's *Design Index*, a resource of Canadian-made products that had the council's seal of approval. The Royal Architectural Institute of Canada's *Allied Art Catalogue 2*, edited by Anita Aarons, also included his work. Drahanchuk's use of indigenous Alberta clays and glazes was lauded – images of the solitary rural potter loomed in the reader's mind. But Drahanchuk was not counting on sales at his local craft fair; rather he produced works that were sold in shops across the country and commissioned for public and corporate spaces. The *Allied Arts Catalogue* featured a ceramic screen in the Shell Oil Building in Toronto and a series of planters destined for Vancouver's futuristic 1968 air terminal. The work of the sixties generation of ceramists and craftspeople – whether it was a vessel, sculpture, or commissioned architectural work – was desired by both the counterculture and the mainstream for its uniqueness.

But no discussion that finds a relationship between the handmade object and the architectural environment is complete without mention of textile work – like the macramé that adorned the temporary living space in the photograph at the beginning of this article. In Sue Scott's wall hanging, the skills of a craftsperson are clearly visible – leaving behind the uneven amateur quality of the work by UBC's architecture students (Figure 8.4). Macramé, based on a knotting

FIGURE 8.4

Sue Scott, wall hanging, c. 1972 (sisal)

COLLECTION OF ONTARIO CRAFTS
COUNCIL, CANADIAN MUSEUM OF
CIVILIZATION, 94-579

PHOTO: HARRY FOSTER, CANADIAN
MUSEUM OF CIVILIZATION

COURTESY OF SUE SCOTT

technique used by sailors, was rediscovered in the sixties by people wanting to produce artworks without having to buy expensive equipment. A ball of twine – from a hardware store, perhaps – was the material of choice. Support for the work could be purchased inexpensively – a simple dowel from a lumberyard – or scrounged – a piece a driftwood or a branch from a tree. But textile work also addressed another aspect of craft production in relation to individual identity – that of gender. Much textile work had been perceived by scholars from as far back as Victorian times as "women's work." Many artists, such as Evelyn Roth with her knitted videotape canopy for the Vancouver Art Gallery in 1973, addressed the place of textile production in contemporaneous society. But macramé's history, with its association with sailors, was more complex. By addressing its complexity and former marginalization, textile work became an expression of individual identity.

The popularization of off-loom techniques and the revived interest in simple traditional dyeing methods allowed for large numbers of the general public to involve themselves in textile crafts as a vehicle for self-expression. Macramé owls and tie-dyed t-shirts flooded craft fairs, folk festivals such as Mariposa, and even shops and department stores across the country. In Vancouver, the Community Arts Council held two Studio Fairs in 1967 and 1968. While many of the council's other initiatives were framed as opportunities to develop the arts in Vancouver, the Studio Fairs were positioned as fundraising opportunities – for craftspeople and the council itself. In a cartoon included in a history of the Community Arts Council, the entrepreneurial aspects of the Studio Fair were satirized (Figure 8.5).[12] But corporate interest in the handmade was more than satirical.

Canadian manufacturers soon took the aesthetic of the handmade and began to produce thousands of identical items with the same "unique" characteristics. Textiles and ceramics manufacturers drew on the popularity of Canada's counterculture activities and devised products that looked as if they were handmade. Members of Canada's counterculture could no longer maintain the aesthetic as their own, since their look had been incorporated into quotidian life and big business. And at the same time that business was appropriating the counterculture's aesthetic, the counterculture itself was beginning to disappear.

The "mixed-up" but "self-possessed" generation had inalterably changed the face of the nation, but by the end of the decade, its idealism had been eclipsed.[13] The "summer of love" of 1967 had been replaced with growing socio-political

"...AND BY COMBINING PHOTOGRAPHY, BATIK AND PRINTMAKING I HOPE TO CREATE, IN MY SMALL WAY, A MONEY-MAKING VENTURE.."

FIGURE 8.5

From: Elizabeth O'Kiely, *The Arts and Our Town: The Community Arts Council of Vancouver, 1946–1996* (Vancouver Community Arts Council, 1996), 50

uncertainty across the country. Protest, which had originally been relatively peaceful, turned violent as unrest grew among youth and more established Canadians. According to the *Toronto Telegram*: "the Flower Children who first bloomed in Yorkville in the summer of 1966 have, like their counterparts in the gardens of the world, surely withered and died."[14]

But those Flower Children of the sixties, those denizens of Canada's counter-culture, still live on through their concerns about the environment and contemporary society. They also live on through the work that they left behind and its influence on mainstream Canada. Those macramé hangings, like the ones made by first-year architecture students at UBC, were only one indication of the rising importance of the individual within a young nation that had expended so much energy on its representation as modern and sophisticated in the earlier years of the decade. The conception of a single idea of nationhood was contested; the idea of Canada became much more complex. Today, this complexity is an integral part of our Canadian identity.

NOTES

INTRODUCTION

1 Pierre Berton, *The Cool, Crazy, Committed World of the Sixties* (Toronto: McClelland and Stewart 1966), xi.

2 Pierre Berton, *1967: The Last Good Year* (Toronto: Doubleday 1997).

3 Peter C. Newman, cited in Geoff Pevere and Craig Dymond, *Mondo Canuck: A Canadian Pop Culture Odyssey* (Scarborough: Prentice-Hall Canada 1996).

4 Geoff Pevere and Craig Dymond, *Mondo Canuck: A Canadian Pop Culture Odyssey* (Scarborough: Prentice-Hall Canada 1996), 135.

5 Lesley Jackson, *The Sixties: Decade of Design Revolution* (London: Phaidon Press, 2000), 135.

6 Berton, *The Cool, Crazy, Committed World*, x.

7 "Canadian Furniture Goes International," *Canadian Homes*, March 1963.

CHAPTER 1

1 *Canadian Architect*, January 1959, 33.

2 Ibid.

3 Ibid.

4 F. Rasky, "Canada's New Temples of Travel," *Canadian Weekly*, 2–8 May 1964, 10–17.

5 D. Sudjic, *The 100 Mile City* (London: HarperCollins 1992), 153–4.

6 P. Smith and B. Toulier, *Airport Architecture of the Thirties* (Paris: Caisse nationale des monuments historiques et des sites Editions du patrimoine 2000), 24.

7 Ken Lum, "Canadian Cultural Policy," *Canadian Art* 16, no. 3 (1999): 76–83.

8 Canada, Royal Commission on National Development in the Arts, Letters and Sciences, Report (Ottawa: King's Printer 1951), Part 2, Introduction, section 2.

9 F. Lowe, "Art in the New Airports Gives Canada a Sophisticated Image," *Canadian Art* 21 (May/June 1964): 144–5.

10 Ibid.

11 Lydia Ferrabee, "Toronto Airport: Interior Design," *Canadian Architect*, February 1964, 63–4.

12 Ibid.

13 Letter from John Gallop of John B. Parkin Associates to Stanley White, Chief Architect's Office, Department of Transport, Ottawa, 5 September 1961.

14 G.L. Lennox, Secretary, Advisory Committee on Fine Arts, to Dr Jean Sutherland Boggs, Director, National Gallery of Canada, 24 May 1968, during the planning of the Vancouver International Airport, National Gallery of Canada Library, Ottawa.

15 A. de Niverville, Circular Letter 2-C57-61, Department of Transport Air Services, 1961.

16 R. Bloom and J. Partridge, "Trouble on Toronto's Tarmac," *Globe and Mail*, 20 March 2004, B5.

17 P. Lucas, "On Wings of Commerce," *Fortune* 149, no. 6 (22 March 2004): 109–20.

CHAPTER 2

1 Some of the ideas discussed in this essay stem from the exhibition *Pop in Orbit: Design from the Space-age*, Design Exchange, 7 September 1995 to 26 February 1996, and *Design in Canada, Fifty Years from Teakettles to Task Chairs* (Toronto: Alfred A. Knopf 2001), which I co-wrote with Cora Golden.

2 Canadian Space Agency, "National Paper, the Canadian Space Program Agency" (19 July 1999); Laurence Mussio, *Telecom Nation: Telecommunications, Computers, and Governments in Canada* (Montreal and Kingston: McGill-Queen's University Press 2001), 43.

3 Mussio, *Telecom Nation*, 105.

4 Interview on 26 February 2004 with Allan Gotlieb, who served as chairman of the Telecommission and deputy minister of DOC between 1968 and 1973.

5 Telecommission, "White Paper: A Domestic Satellite Communication System for Canada" (Ottawa, 1967); Mussio, *Telecom Nation*, 194.

6 *Instant World: A Report on Telecommunications in Canada* (Ottawa: Information Canada 1971), 90.

7 Marshall McLuhan, quoted from *Telecom Nation*, 189.

8 *Time*, 4 September 1964, 83.

9 For a discussion on pop, see Nigel Whiteley, *Pop Design – Modernism to Mod* (London: Design Council 1987); Lesley Jackson, *The Sixties: Decade of Design Revolution* (London: Phaidon 1999).

10 Electrohome marketing brochures, Design Exchange.

11 Electrohome case study in a 1973 Design Canada unpublished report, 2–3, Design Exchange.

12 Design Canada unpublished report, 1.

13 Mussio, *Telecom Nation*, 157.

CHAPTER 3

1 Quoted in Rick Archbold, *I Stand for Canada: The Story of the Maple Leaf Flag* (Toronto: Macfarlane Walter and Ross 2000), 4.

2 John Ross Matheson, *Canada's Flag: A Search for a Country* (Belleville, Ont.: Mika 1986).

3 Eric Hobsbawm and Terence Ranger, eds, *The Invention of Tradition* (Cambridge: Cambridge University Press 1983), 11–13.

4 Philippe Garner, *Sixties Design* (Köln: Taschen 1996), 8.

5 Reyner Banham, "A Throw-Away Aesthetic," reprinted in *Design by Choice*, edited by Penny Sparke (New York: Rizzoli 1981), 93.

6 A valuable account of the period, and of the rival claims to the authorship of the CN logo, can be found in Brian Donnelly, *Graphic Design in Canada since 1945* (Ottawa: Carleton University Art Gallery 1996).

7 *Canadian Art* 20, no. 5 (September/October 1963): 272–5.

8 Archbold, *I Stand for Canada* and Matheson, *Canada's Flag*.

9 Matheson, *Canada's Flag*, gives a thorough account.

10 Alan Way, "The Government of Canada's Federal Identity Program," *Design Management Journal* (Design Management Institute, Boston), 4, no. 3 (Summer 1993): 55–62; and Michael Large, "The Corporate Identity of the Canadian Government," *Journal of Design History* (Oxford University Press), 4, no. 1 (1991): 31–42.

11 Naomi Klein, *No Logo: Taking Aim at the Brand Bullies* (Toronto: Knopf Canada 2000).

CHAPTER 4

1 Mavor Moore, "Lives Lived: Moncrieff Williamson," *Globe and Mail*, 2 September 1996, National Gallery of Canada Archives, DOC/CLWT Williamson, Moncrieff 1915–1996.

2 *Biography of Moncrieff Williamson*, file: Canadian Conference of the Arts, Prince Edward Island Archives (PEIA), Moncrieff Williamson Archives, RG 44 S.2, box 25.

3 Moore, "Lives Lived: Moncrieff Williamson."

4 Moncrieff Williamson, "The New Museums and Art Galleries: 1967 and After," file: Canadian Conference of the Arts, PEIA, Moncrieff Williamson Archives, RG 44 S.2, box 25.

5 Mary Eileen Muff, "Report from the Meeting of Canadian Craftsmen," Winnipeg, 5–7 February 1965, Archives of Ontario, Ontario Crafts Council, Archives of Canadian Craft, MU5750, box 5, BU-BW2. The original name for the Canadian Craftsmen's Association was the Canadian Council for the Environmental Arts/Conseil Canadien pour les arts de l'espace, a title suggested by Arnold Rockman, then editor of the journal *Canadian Art*.

6 These craftspeople were Lois (and Foster) Beveridge, stoneware jug and bowl in ash glaze; Merton Chambers, terra cotta mosaic wall plaque; Walter Dexter, stoneware vase; Beth Hone, stoneware garden light; Ludwig Nickel, *Growth of a Nation*, marble base, enamel top; Helga Palko, pin with pearl, sterling silver; Jack Sures, stoneware bowl and stoneware plate.

7 Norah McCullough, letter to Moncrieff Williamson, 12 October 1965, file: Expo 67 General – 1965, PEIA, Moncrieff Williamson Archives, RG 44, S.2, box 82. Dorothy Todd Hénaut promoted Williamson's *Canadian Fine Crafts* in her article "1967 – The Moment of Truth for Canadian Crafts," published in *ArtsCanada* 24, no. 104 (January 1967): 20–2. Hénaut, who mailed Williamson a copy of her article to edit, wrote: "In sum, it will be the epitome of contemporary Canadian crafts."

8 Moncrieff Williamson, letter to Leslie Brown, commissioner general, Canadian Government Pavilion 1967 Exhibition, 4 October 1964, file: Expo 67 General – 1965, PEIA, Moncrieff Williamson Archives, RG 44, S.2, box 82.

9 McCullough, letter to Williamson, 12 October 1965.

10 Moncrieff Williamson, *Canadian Fine Crafts* (Ottawa: Queen's Printers 1967), 4, Thomas Fisher Rare Book Library, University of Toronto, T-1015 Collection of Miscellaneous Material on Expo 67. The catalogue contained biographical material on the artists, including their place of birth and locations of formal training. Of the

120 exhibitors, 95 (79 per cent) had received professional craft education. Of those with professional training, 79 per cent had received their education in Canada, with 27 per cent of those educated in Canada receiving their training in Quebec. A further 32 per cent had attended school or apprenticed overseas (mainly in Europe), while 19 per cent had attended a craft school in the United States.

11 <http://www.kennedy-center.org/about/gifts/canada.htm>.

12 Moncrieff Williamson, letter to Duncan de Kergommeaux, gallery director, Canadian Pavilion, 7 August 1967, file: Crafts Museum Correspondence, PEIA, Moncrieff Williamson Archives, RG 44, S.2, box 25.

13 Minutes of the second meeting of the Fine Arts Advisory Committee of the Canadian Government Committee, 1967 Exhibition, 15 June 1964, 4, file: Expo 67 General – 1965, PEIA, Moncrieff Williamson Archives, RG 44, S.2, box 82.

14 Paul Schoeler, architect, letter to Moncrieff Williamson, 14 December 1965, file: Expo 67 General – 1965, PEIA, Moncrieff Williamson Archives, RG 44, S.2, box 82.

15 "Expo a Storehouse of World's Treasure," *Montreal Star*, 28 April 1967: 66, Metropolitan Toronto Reference Library Archive, folio 909.82607E88, Expo 67.

16 Williamson, *Canadian Fine Crafts*, 11. One could speculate that such a marked use of stoneware was linked to the influence of Bernard Leach, Michael Cardew, and Michael Casson, and to the use of stoneware in the back-to-the-land movement of the sixties.

17 "Sees Opportunity for P.E.I. Craftsmen," 1965, newspaper clipping from Confederation Centre scrapbook on Robert Harris, possibly from the *Evening Patriot*.

18 Norah McCullough, "Report to Craftsmen," memo for *World Crafts Council Newsletter*, 31 August 1967; National Archives of Canada, MG28I274, vol. 33, World Crafts Council.

19 Sandra Flood, *Canadian Craft and Museum Practice 1900–1950* (Gatineau: Canadian Museum of Civilization 2001), 281.

20 Ibid., 276.

21 Ellen Easton McLeod, *In Good Hands: The Women of the Canadian Handicrafts Guild* (Montreal and Kingston: McGill-Queen's University Press for Carleton University 1999), 286.

22 "Sees Opportunity for P.E.I. Craftsmen."

23 Ibid.

24 *After 1967, What? An Epilogue* (Seminar 67 Canadian Conference of the Arts report), 16, file: Canadian Conference of the Arts, PEIA, Moncrieff Williamson Archives, RG 44, S.2, box 25

25 Kevin Rice, registrar and associate curator, Confederation Centre Art Gallery, personal interview, 28 January 2004, Charlottetown, P.E.I. Although these works were incorporated into the collection, they retain the marking "CM" that originally numbered them for craft museum.

26 Easton McLeod, *In Good Hands*, 286.

27 Memorandum Regarding a National Museum of Crafts and Design, Canadian Crafts Council, 1 September 1982, file: Special Projects Committee – 1022-6 National Gallery of Crafts and Design, National Archives of Canada, Canadian Crafts Council, MG 28, I 274, vol. 87.

28 Williamson, *Canadian Fine Crafts*, 12.

CHAPTER 5

1 Hubert Beringer, "Habitat 67: Architectures d'images, images d'architectures," *Journal de la Société pour l'étude de l'architecture au Canada* 27, nos 1, 2 (2002): 3–20.

2 Ibid., 4 (translation).

3 Ibid., 16.

4 Two lighting fixtures are among the products illustrated in *Canadian Design at Expo 67/ Le Design canadien à l'Expo 67* (Ottawa: National Design Council, 1968), nos 105, 108.

5 Doris Giller, "Architect Consults Wife on Kitchen," *Montreal Star*, 24 July 1965.

6 "Un réfrigérateur qui se déplace facilement!" *La Presse*, 14 April 1967.

7 See *Canadian Design at Expo 67*, no. 100.

8 Moshe Safdie, *Beyond Habitat* (Montreal: Tundra Books, 1970), 107.

9 In a radio interview, a "user" expressed a few reservations, however, pointing out that cleaning was difficult (CBC Archives, *Expodition*, 25 October 1967, Bob McGregor interview with Mr and Mrs Robin Randall).

10 "Habitat '67 Makes First Mass Use of Prefabricated Bathrooms," *Heating/Plumbing/air conditioning* 45, no. 11 (13 June 1966): 1. See also several articles in the construction magazines of the time: *Building Material News*, June 1966; *Building Management*, June 1966; and *Building Supply Dealer*, July 1966. These are the same images that appear in "Habitat 67, Montréal," *L'Architecture d'Aujourd'hui* 38, no. 130 (February–March 1967): 28–30; and Alexander Pike, "Habitat '67," *Architectural Design* 37, no. 3 (March 1967): 111–19.

11 *Expo 67 Official Guide* (Toronto, Montreal: Maclean-Hunter, 1967), 17.

12 John Bland Canadian Architecture Collection (CAC), Rare Books and Special Collections Division, McGill University Libraries, Fonds Moshe Safdie, CAC58/100/PF1/14, *Habitat House Exhibits*, "Minutes of 1st Meeting 'Habitat Exhibition Use Committee,'" 4 May 1965.

13 CAC, Fonds Moshe Safdie, CAC58/100/PF1/14, *Habitat House Exhibits*, "Summary of recommendations by the Habitat Exhibition Use Committee," 23 August 1965.

14 This committee was made up of representatives from the Canadian Council of Furniture Manufacturers, Vilas Industries Ltd, Harding Carpets Ltd, Dominion Electrohome Industry Ltd, Frigidaire Products of Canada, Fiberglass Canada Ltd, and T. Eaton & Company.

15 "Expo Challenges Furniture Makers," *Home Goods Retailing*, 18 April 1966. See also "Habitat Furnishings," *Canadian Interiors* 3, no. 6 (June 1966): 22; "L'Industrie canadienne meublera 'Habitat 67,'" *Montréal-Matin*, 21 July 1966.

16 CAC, Fonds Moshe Safdie, CAC58/100/PF1/14, *Habitat House Exhibits*, draft letter from Édouard Fiset to Colonel Edward Churchill, "Furnishing of Exhibit Units – Habitat '67," 20 April 1966.

17 Information provided by Jacques Guillon, 4 June 2004.

18 Safdie, *Beyond Habitat*, 135.

19 CAC, Fonds Moshe Safdie, CAC58/100/PF1/14, *Habitat House Exhibits*, personal letter from Moshe Safdie to Erik Herlow (Danish architect), 15 August 1966.

20 Charles Lazarus, "All-Canadian Decision Disputed. Can't Furnish Habitat, Dane Disappointed," *Montreal Star*, 6 September 1966; and "Expo Steering Committee Meets in Moscow. Habitat to Stay All Canadian – Including Furniture," *Montreal Star*, 13 September 1966.

21 CAC, Fonds Moshe Safdie, CAC58/100/PF1/14, *Habitat House Exhibits*, "Technical Brief," 16 June 1966.

22 For an example of *Chatelaine*'s proposals, see the reproduction of its models in the *Telegram* (Toronto), 26 August 1966.

23 CAC, Fonds Moshe Safdie, CAC58/100/PF1/14, *Habitat House Exhibits*, letter from Jacques Guillon to Édouard Fiset, 1 November 1966.

24 CAC, Fonds Moshe Safdie, CAC58/100/PF1/14, *Habitat House Exhibits*, personal letter from Moshe Safdie to Erik Herlow (Danish architect), 18 November 1966, and letter from Jacques Guillon and Moshe Safdie to Colonel Edward Churchill, 21 November 1966.

25 CAC, Fonds Moshe Safdie, CAC58/100/PF1/14, *Habitat House Exhibits*, letter from Anthony A. Peters to Moshe Safdie, 8 September 1966.

26 Doris Giller "'Garden-in-the-sky' Interior Furnishings Unveiled," *Montreal Star*, 8 February 1967; Leo MacGillivray, "Habitat Homes Bright, Well Furnished," *Saturday Gazette*, 11 February 1967; and Lyse Rossignol, "Habitat '67 : un coûteux écrin qui contient de la pacotille," *La Presse*, 9 February 1967. The latter observed, noting the revealing absence of Moshe Safdie, that "[i]t is inexcusable that the authorities of the World Fair permitted such lack of care in the decoration of an ultra-modern building, hastily furnished rooms such as one finds in all the ordinary furnished apartments or the motels on the outskirts of the metropolis." But, according to the journalist, there was hope, since "thirteen other [houses] will be beautified with avant-garde creations by our best designers and interior decorators" (translation).

27 "12 Habitat Suites," *Canadian Interiors* 4, no. 9 (September 1967): 79.

28 Information provided by Alison Hymas, 16 June 2004.

29 An article in *Canadian Homes* mentioned two other contributions, furniture with architectural lines by Keith Muller and Michael Stewart and collapsible furniture by Macy Dubois. But it appears that these designs were not part of the twelve suites in Concept B of Habitat. Margaret Marden, "Canadian Furniture Designers," *Canadian Homes*, September 1967, 8.

30 See *Canadian Design at Expo 67*, no. 95.

31 Information provided by Michel Dallaire, 9 June 2004.

32 See Margaret Marden, "Canadian Furniture Designers," cover page; and *Canadian Design at Expo 67*, no. 76.

33 See *Canadian Design at Expo 67*, nos 70–1.

34 Ibid., no. 42.

35 Nicole Benoit, "Qui sont ces chaises?" *Décormag* 3, no. 6 (February 1975): 18.

36 "Dal Canada," *Domus*, no. 532 (March 1974): 41.

37 "12 Habitat Suites," 39.

38 See *Canadian Design at Expo 67*, nos 41, 58, 87, 106.

39 Information provided by Jerry Adamson, 9 June 2004.

40 "Exciting Uses of Plastic," *Canadian Interiors* 4, no. 11 (November 1967): 47.

41 Suzanne Morrison, "The Couple of the Future: They'll Rent Furniture Too," *Toronto Daily Star*, 7 April 1967.

42 DuBarry Campeau, "Chairs Light Your Patio," *Telegram*, 7 April 1967.

43 Rachel Gotlieb and Cora Golden, *Design in Canada since 1945: Fifty Years from Teakettles to Task Chairs* (Toronto: Alfred A. Knopf Canada and Design Exchange, 2001), 101.

44 "12 Habitat Suites," 49.

45 *Canadian Interiors* 4, no. 8 (August 1967).

46 *Canadian Design at Expo 67*, nos 53, 78, 83, 86, 103; and "12 Habitat Suites," 40.

47 "Fold This Plywood Furniture, Re-Assemble It without Tools," *Financial Post*, 6 May 1967.

48 *Canadian Design at Expo 67*, nos 59, 66; "12 Habitat Suites," 47; and Eleanor Callaghan, "Canadian Made Furniture Easy to Put Together," *Montreal Star*, 25 April 1967.

49 "12 Habitat Suites," 46; and for the draft letter from Sigrun Bülow-Hübe to D. Piper from *Canadian Interiors*, see CAC, Fonds Sigrun Bülow-Hübe, CAC65/BP/5/ Expo/1.01.

50 See *Canadian Design at Expo 67*, nos 62, 64, 65, 67, 68, 77, 79, 84, 91, 92, 93, 96, 104.

51 See *Canadian Design at Expo 67*, nos 63, 81, 89, 90; and "12 Habitat Suites," 52.

52 See *Canadian Design at Expo 67*, nos 60, 61.

53 "Creative Office Furniture Design a Victim of Needless Compromise," *Stationery and Office Products*, January 1967.

CHAPTER 6

1 Nikolaus Pevsner, *High Victorian Design: A Study of the Exhibits of 1851* (London: Architectural Press 1951), 17.

2 Thomas Hancock, *Personal Narrative of the Origin and Progress of the Caoutchouc or India-Rubber Manufacture in England* (London: Longman, Brown, Green, Longmans, & Roberts 1857), 129–30.

3 Rev. Bradford K. Peirce, *Trials of an Inventor: Life and Discoveries of Charles Goodyear* (New York: Carlton & Porter 1866), 168.

4 P.W. Barker, *Charles Goodyear: Connecticut Yankee and Rubber Pioneer* (Boston: Godfrey I.. Cabot 1940), 61–2.

5 Ibid.

6 Peirce, *Trials of an Inventor*, 169.

7 Josef Strasser, "From War to the Economic Miracle: The Fifties," in *Plastics Design +* (Munich: Arnoldsche Art Publishers 1997), 55.

8 Christy Borth, *Modern Chemists and Their Works* (New York: New Home Library 1943), 207.

9 E.G. Cousins et al., *Plastics in the Modern World* (Middlesex: Penguin Books 1968), 346.

10 Kathryn B. Hiesinger et al., *Landmarks of Twentieth Century Design: An Illustrated Handbook* (New York: Abbeville Press Publishers 1993), 151.

11 O.T. Zimmerman et al., *Handbook of Material Trade Names* (Dover: Industrial Research Service 1959).

12 George Kateb, "Utopia and the Good Life," *Utopias and Utopian Thought: A Timely Appraisal* (Boston: Beacon Press 1966), 239.

13 Penny Sparke, "Plastics and Pop Culture," in *The Plastics Age: From Bakelite to Beanbags and Beyond*, edited by Penny Sparke (New York: Overlook Press 1992), 93.

14 Arthur Drexler, "The Package," *Museum of Modern Art Bulletin* 27, no. 1 (New York: MOMA 1959), 8.

15 Ibid.

16 Hal Foster, "On the First Pop Age," *New Left Review* 19 (January–February 2003) http://www.newleftreview.net/NLR25306.shtml.

17 Sparke, "Plastics and Pop Culture," 94.

18 R. Buckminster Fuller, *Utopia or Oblivion: The Prospects for Humanity* (New York: Bantam Books 1969), 272–4.

19 Ibid.

20 Ibid.

21 Ibid.

22 Josef Strasser, "Utopias in Plastic: The Euphoria of Synthetic Materials in the Sixties and Early Seventies," in *Plastics Design +* (Munich: Arnoldsche Art Publishers 1997), 85.

23 Hiesinger et al., *Landmarks of Twentieth Century Design*, 249.

24 Marc Dessauce, "On Pneumatic Apparitions," in *The Inflatable Moment: Pneumatics and Protest in '68*, edited by Marc Dessauce (New York: Princeton Architectural Press 1999), 15.

CHAPTER 7

1 *The Decorators' Show* (Toronto: n.p., 1958), 16.

2 For a useful discussion of the arrival of material modernism in Canada, see Virginia Wright, *Modern Furniture in Canada, 1920 to 1970* (Toronto: University of Toronto Press 1997).

3 The idea of a modern Canada emerging in the postwar decades was powerfully shown in an advertisement run by Maclean-Hunter in late 1967. Titled "Builders of a New Canada in a New World," the ad featured a stylized drawing of Toronto and Montreal (the former signified by two Meisien towers and the latter by Place Ville Marie and other downtown skyscrapers). Linking the cities were freeways and swooping access ramps. Above the cloverleaf was an image of a busy factory with smokestacks, and below the highway was a railway bridge over a river. The text was

equally celebratory: "Conceived in dreams, accomplished in imagination and authority, the new Canada rises around us." Indeed, what with "great rivers" being "stopped in their course and made to yield energy for making things and moving people" and "the shabby cores of great cities" being "rebuilt into exciting centres of commerce with magnificent skylines," there was palpable evidence of what Maclean-Hunter regarded as the "dazzling spectacle of Canadians building a New Canada" (*Canadian Interiors*, November 1967, 24).

4 For an excellent analysis of the ways that Canadians negotiated material modernity, see Joy Parr, *Domestic Goods: The Material, the Moral and the Economic in the Postwar Years* (Toronto: University of Toronto Press 1999). See especially 121–64.

5 See, for example, the advertisement for the new "colonial collections" of furniture of Gibbard's of Napanee. Named the "Quinte Collection" and available in cherry, the pieces were "inspired by the heirlooms of United Empire Loyalists had who settled near Napanee in the Bay of Quinte area." Comprised of "bedroom, dining and living room groupings" and available with "fascinating authentic accessories," the collection was designed to help homemakers "recreate the ageless warmth and charm of the early Canadian colonial days" (*Canadian Homes and Gardens*, May 1962, 1).

For another striking, albeit late-1950s, example of the types of traditional furniture available to Canadian consumers, see the advertisement for Simpson's "Pilgrim Rock Maple" (*Canadian Homes and Gardens*, April 1958, 16). See also Hespeler's advertisement for its line of French provincial furniture and Thibault's promotion of their "living, liveable" furniture with its historical sensitive styling and alleged timelessness (*Canadian Homes and Gardens*, August 1960, 34, and August 1961, 7).

6 *Western Homes and Living*, March 1965, 27.

7 This theme is revealed powerfully in a 1957 advertisement for Deilcraft where the text explains that the company's "new Scandia Group" available at Simpson's "has drawn from the clean sweeping lines of Scandinavian design for inspiration" (*Canadian Homes and Gardens*, August 1960, 34).

8 *Canadian Homes and Gardens*, January 1962, 55.

9 *Canadian Homes and Gardens*, July 1962, 7.

10 *Canadian Homes and Gardens*, June 1962, 54–5.

11 Ibid.

12 "It's Always Open House at the Harringtons'" *Canadian Homes and Gardens*, June 1962, 32–3.

13 *Western Homes and Living*, October 1966, 72.

14 See, for example, *Canadian Homes and Gardens*, August 1961.

CHAPTER 8

1 A.M.R. Lower, *Colony to Nation: A History of Canada* (Toronto: Longmans, Green 1946).

2 Jon Ruddy, "Stop the world – they want to get off," *Maclean's*, 1 November 1965, 21.

3 In 1967 it was reported that 19,038 U.S. citizens moved to Canada, thereby offsetting the perceived "brain drain" (Ruddy, "Stop the world," 21).

4 Myrna Kostach, *Long Way from Home* (Toronto: James Lorimer, 1980), 118 f.

5 In part, this may be attributed in Canada to the attention paid to historical Canadian furniture during the centennial celebrations of 1967.

6 Kostach, *Long Way from Home*, 121

7 From "For What It's Worth" by Stephen Stills.

8 "Craft Dimensions," *Canadian Art*, September 1969.

9 Gail Crawford, *A Fine Line: Studio Crafts in Ontario from 1930 to Present* (Toronto: Dundurn Press 1998), 113.

10 Karen White, *Donald Lloyd McKinley: A Studio Practice in Furniture* (Oakville, Ont.: Oakville Galleries 2000), 19.

11 "The happy emergence of people power," *Maclean's*, January 1969, 21.

12 Elizabeth O'Kiely, *The Arts and Our Town: The Community Arts Council 1946–1996* (Vancouver: Community Arts Council 1996), 50.

13 Pierre Burton, *The Cool, Crazy, Committed World of the Sixties* (Toronto: McClelland and Stewart 1966), xi

14 *Telegram* (Toronto), 22 April 1970, 7.

This book was designed and typeset by Garet Markvoort
of zijn digital in Montreal and printed and bound by
Friesens of Altona, Manitoba.

The text is set in 10.5/14 Cartier Book, a digital version of
the typeface Cartier. Cartier was created by typographer
Carl Dair in 1967 to celebrate Canada's centennial and the
Montreal World's Fair. It was the first text typeface designed
in Canada. Cartier Book is the work of Canadian designer
Rod McDonald and was released by Agfa-Monotype in 2000.

The display face is Gill Sans, designed by Eric Gill and first
issued by Monotype between 1928 and 1932. The digital
version used here is from Adobe Systems.

The paper is Garda Silk. It is acid-free and of archival quality.